Political and Economic Systems
CAPITALISM

David Downing

Heinemann Library
Chicago, Illinois

© 2008 Heinemann Library
a division of Reed Elsevier Inc.
Chicago, Illinois

Customer Service 888-454-2279
Visit our website at www.heinemannraintree.com

Designed by Richard Parker and Q2A Creative
Printed and bound in China by South China Printing Company

12 11 10 09 08
10 9 8 7 6 5 4 3 2 1

New edition ISBN: 978-1-4329-0231-5 (hardcover)
                    978-1-4329-0756-3 (paperback)

**The Library of Congress has catalogued the first
edition as follows:**
Downing, David.
      Capitalism / David Downing.
         p. cm. -- (Political and economic systems)
Includes bibliographical references and index.
      ISBN 1-40340-315-5
      1. Capitalism -- Juvenile literature. [1. Capitalism]
      I. Title. II. Series.
      HB501 .D684 2003
      330.12'2--dc21

                        2002006316

Acknowledgments
The publishers would like to thank the following for permission to reproduce photographs:
Bridgeman/Bristol Museum: p. 8; Corbis: p. 21; Corbis Sygma/Bob Daemmrich: p. 46; Corbis/
Bettmann: pp. 10, 11, 23, 24, 33; Corbis/Charles O'Rear: p. 38; Corbis/David and Peter
Turnley: p. 39; Corbis/Eye Ubiquitous: p. 50; Corbis/Gianni Dagli Orti: p. 7; Corbis/Keren
Su: p. 52; Corbis/Michael S. Yamashita: p. 49; Corbis/Philip de Bay: p. 13; Rex Features/Sipa
Press: p. 54; Corbis/Tony Arruza: p. 44; Corbis/Wally McNamee: p. 30; Getty Images/ Hulton:
pp. 16, 17, 18, 21, 26, 29, 36, 41; Hulton Archive/Dorothea Lange: p. 21; Master file/ Hans
Blohm: p. 43; Rex/Andy Hernandez: p. 34; Rex/Nick Cobbins: p. 5

Cover photograph of a skyscraper in Dallas, Texas, USA, reproduced with permission
of Robert Harding/Steve Bavister. Background image reproduced with permission of
istockphoto.com/Kristen Johansen

Every effort has been made to contact copyright holders of any material reproduced in
this book. Any omissions will be rectified in subsequent printings if notice is given to the
publishers.

Our thanks to Christopher Gibb and Stewart Ross for their comments in the preparation of
this book.

Disclaimer
All the Internet addresses (URLs) given in this book were valid at the time of going to press.
However, due to the dynamic nature of the Internet, some addresses may have changed, or
sites may have changed or ceased to exist since publication. While the author and publishers
regret any inconvenience this may cause readers, no responsibility for any such changes can
be accepted by either the author or the publishers.

Contents

Any words appearing in the text in bold, **like this**, are explained in the glossary.

The Specter at the Feast

It was the last day of November 1999, and the new millennium was only a month away. Ten years earlier, the power of world communism had collapsed, leaving the economic system known as capitalism in triumphant control of most of the globe. For more than two centuries, capitalism had dominated the economic life of an ever-increasing number of countries, piling up untold riches in the process. People in the countries of the developed West were roughly 20 times better off than their ancestors had been in the 1750s.

There was surely nothing to complain about. Hadn't capitalism delivered the goods and the good life better than anyone could have dared to expect? Yet on this day, in the city of Seattle, a rich city in the world's richest country, a large protest was taking place. A protest against capitalism.

The protesters marched in the thousands, down streets lined with stores full of products from all around the world, of every conceivable description. They marched in the shadows of modern skyscrapers, which stood like testaments to capitalism's growth and prosperity. This was Seattle, famous for the TV sitcom *Frasier* and rock bands like Nirvana and Pearl Jam, proof that capitalism encouraged freedom and creativity. If any place on Earth had been truly blessed by capitalism, then surely this was it. So why were these men and women marching?

Their banners told a confused story. Many were protesting against the **World Trade Organization**, whose meeting in the city had triggered the protest. Some carried signs condemning a general lack of justice and fairness in the world. Others had more particular targets in mind—logging companies that were cutting down forests, junk food chains that seemed to be spreading like a virus around the world, industries that used animals to test the safety of their products. In the marchers' minds, all these issues were connected. As one Internet website that advertised the event had described it, this was a global day of action, resistance, and a party against the global capitalist system.

No one doubted that capitalism had filled the stores with products and built the towering skyscrapers, but was it also responsible for the various problems and injustices that made the protesters so angry? What exactly was capitalism? Where had it come from, and how had it changed during the centuries of its rise to global domination? Why were some of those who had reaped its rewards so excited to challenge it—or even to see it destroyed?

Police and protesters confront each other on the streets of Seattle in November 1999. The protester's sign accuses the World Trade Organization (**WTO**) of being undemocratic.

Where Did Capitalism Come From?

Capitalism is an economic system—a system deciding how goods and services are produced and traded. It has three key features: most property is owned by individuals; goods and services are exchanged in a competitive **free market** (one that is open to everyone); and **capital** (either money or other forms of wealth) is **invested** in businesses in order to make a **profit**—an increase in the wealth that was invested. Capitalism did not make a sudden appearance in world history, but developed through several centuries, its importance growing within certain key societies until it came to dominate their economic life.

The seeds of capitalism

People have always owned things, markets for trading goods have existed almost as long, and capital goods of both types—**working capital** and **fixed capital**—could be found on any primitive farm. The seeds saved from one year's harvest were the farmer's working capital, the raw material out of which he would create the next year's harvest. The hoe he used to plant those seeds was the farmer's fixed capital, the thing he needed to make the best use of his working capital. However, he was not using this capital to make a profit, only to feed himself and his family.

Attitudes toward the creation of wealth

Traditional attitudes toward the creation of wealth were often hostile. The Bible said that, "...he who maketh haste [hurries] to be rich shall not be innocent" (Proverbs chapter 28, verse 20). The Koran disapproved of taking interest on loans, and other religions had similar reservations about profit. The influence of such beliefs lessened as capitalism became the dominant economic system, but as late as 1948 the Indian political and religious leader Mohandas Gandhi could say that someone who charged as much as he possibly could for goods was no better than a thief. Such attitudes are still strongly held in some circles.

By ancient Greek and Roman times, there were an increasing number of merchants and traders using their fixed capital (a string of camels, perhaps) and working capital (a shipment of silk, maybe) to make a profit.

For several more centuries, such people played only a small part in the overall economy. The odds were stacked against people like this becoming more important. In medieval Europe, organizations of craftspeople and traders, called guilds, decided what the prices and wages would be in their towns, and this made it impossible for individuals to compete with each other by selling their goods or labor more cheaply. There was also widespread religious prejudice against money lending, which made it difficult for anyone to raise the capital needed to start or expand businesses. Those who did make profits tended to spend them on things like fine clothes and impressive houses, rather than using their money to make even more.

A medieval manuscript showing an official from the Guild of Wool Merchants paying a weaver for his cloth. The Guild controlled the weavers' rates of pay.

Commercial capitalism

Slowly but surely, as trade increased and the use of money spread, the small pockets of capitalistic activity in northern and western Europe grew in number and importance. In the 15th and 16th centuries, the vast expansion of trade that followed the opening up of routes to Asia and the newly discovered Americas introduced what became known as the age of commercial capitalism (commerce is another word for trade). Most of the capital was still working capital—the goods filling the ships now criss-crossing the oceans—but there was also a large increase in those types of fixed capital that the new trade needed: things like ships and dock facilities.

During the same period, there was an increase in the making of cloth in private homes. Merchants would deliver raw wool (the working capital) to households where primitive machines (the fixed capital) would be used to turn it into cloth. Such arrangements were like a halfway house on the road to full capitalism. Two hundred years later, these part-time home workers would be working full-time for a wage in heavily supervised factories.

This painting shows Bristol, England in 1720. Ports such as Bristol grew prosperous as world trade expanded under capitalism.

A more favorable climate

As capitalism's importance to the economies of these European countries grew, people's attitudes toward money and the creation of wealth also changed. Governments began to encourage their merchants and traders, and to support them actively against the merchants and traders of other countries. Businesspeople grew more popular as the older ruling class— the land-owning **aristocracy**—grew less popular. By the time of the European **Enlightenment**, which valued logical thinking above tradition, the climate for capitalism looked brighter.

Capitalism had been helped by the rise of **Protestantism** during the 16th century **Reformation**. Protestants believed that nature was there to be tamed, that hard work and saving were virtuous things to do, and that wealth was a reward from God. Such attitudes helped capitalism flourish. It seems unlikely that the simultaneous triumphs of capitalism and Protestantism were a coincidence, but historians have disagreed about the exact nature of the connection.

The Industrial Revolution

In the 18th century, capitalism's takeover was sped up even more by the series of inventions and technical advances that historians came to call the **Industrial Revolution**. The first industry to be transformed was the British textile industry. The invention and spread of new machines such as Hargreaves' spinning-jenny (which could spin wool into yarn) and Arkwright's water frame (which used river power to drive a large spinning wheel) transformed what had been a part-time, domestic activity—typically, women working at home—into a factory job.

The ability to make cheap cloth meant enormous profits for those who owned the machines, and they invested these profits into new machines for making more cloth. Traditional cloth producers, both in Britain and elsewhere, struggled to compete, and by 1850 the United Kingdom's factories were making half the world's cotton goods.

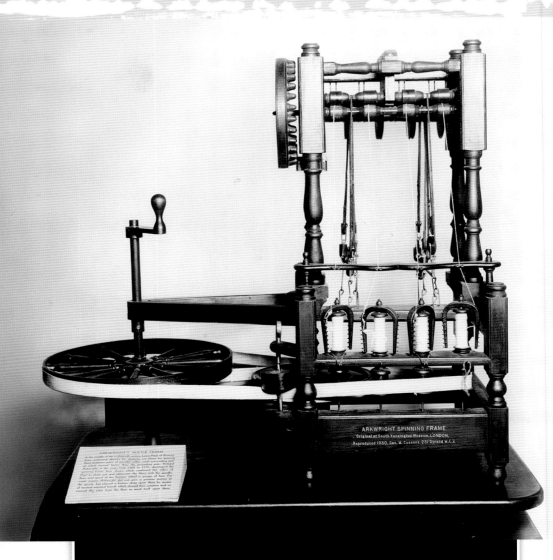

This machine is a replica of the spinning frame invented by Richard Arkwright in the 18th century. It could spin wool into yarn much quicker than previous methods.

The same was true in industry after industry. The fixed capital of the late 18th and early 19th centuries—mines, ironworks, potteries—spread across the landscape of North America and Europe, turning working capital into profits. These were reinvested in more capital, which made more profits, and so on. By the mid-19th century, capitalism was the dominant force in all Western economies.

Building Prosperity

In the late 18th century, the Scottish **philosopher** and economist Adam Smith wrote a book called *An Inquiry into the Nature and Causes of the Wealth of Nations*. In this book he explained how capitalism worked and why he believed it worked in the interest of everyone, not just those fortunate enough to own capital. If certain conditions were met, he said, if most property was private and people were able to choose between competing buyers and sellers in a free market, then one person's pursuit of profit would end up benefiting not just himself, but the whole community. What Smith called the invisible hand of the market would work in everyone's interests.

How capitalism works

Why would one person's profit not be someone else's loss? According to Smith, it worked something like this. A businessman—businesswomen were almost unheard of—would borrow the money to buy the machines that he needed to set up a factory for making, say, wool blankets.

Adam Smith (1723–90) was a Scottish economist and philosopher. Many people consider him to be the founder of modern economics.

The cost of making each blanket—what he had to pay out—would include **interest payments** on his loan, wages to his workers, rent or mortgage on his factory, energy costs, and expenditures (what he spent) on raw materials such as wool and dyes. In order to make a profit he had to charge his customers more for his blankets than the amount it cost him to make them.

So why would this businessman not charge twice the cost and make a huge profit? Adam Smith's answer was simple—he could not do so because he was competing in a free market with other blanket manufacturers. If he raised his prices too high, and tried to make too much profit, then people would buy blankets from his rivals, who were charging less. Competition kept prices down.

In order to compete, the businessman was involved in a relentless effort to keep his costs down. It was in his interest to make his blanket business more efficient by using better machines and fewer workers. If he did not, and his competitors did, then he would be unable to sell his own over-priced blankets.

This search for profit drove the entire machine forward. Businessmen in every industry struggled to undercut their competitors by finding new ways of making things, new things to make, new markets at home and abroad to sell them in, anything at all to give them an advantage. The outcome was a whole new world of mass-produced, affordable products.

The golden age

During the first half of the 19th century, capitalism developed much as Smith had predicted it would. Most businesses were owned by the individuals or families who ran them, and not, as is usually the case today, by thousands of shareholders who play little part in day-to-day operations. Enterprises were also small by today's standards, and the fierce and open competition between them benefited the consumer.

The people of the time respected savings, which encouraged investment, and they also admired those who were prepared to take the risk of trying something new, which encouraged innovation.

This was the golden age of capitalism. In 1851, the Great Exhibition was held in London to celebrate the progress that had been made. Thousands came to see the amazing machines that had transformed the way people lived. Even capitalism's enemies were stunned by the enormity of the changes. Three years earlier, in their **Communist** *Manifesto*, Karl Marx and Friedrich Engels had written that "capitalism, during its rule of scarce [barely] one hundred years, has created more massive and more colossal productive forces [forces that help make things] than have all preceding generations together."

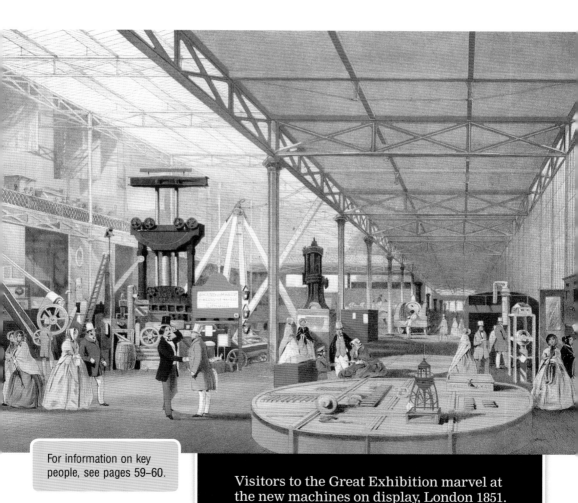

For information on key people, see pages 59–60.

Visitors to the Great Exhibition marvel at the new machines on display, London 1851.

There was no slowing the pace as the 19th century merged with the 20th. The rise of new industries based on oil and electricity, the development of automobiles and manned flight, all changed the face of the land and the way people lived their lives. By the time World War I broke out in August 1914, only small pockets of the old, slow-moving, pre-industrial world still existed in North America and Europe. In its place, capitalism had built a prosperous world of cities and fast machines, a world in which fast-growing economies went hand in hand with spreading education, widening **democracy**, and flourishing culture.

Stock markets and shareholders

Businessmen often needed extra capital to make their businesses grow faster. At the same time there were many private investors with small amounts of capital who were interested in making a profit. So a system grew up in which businessmen sold the investors shares in their businesses, and paid them a share of whatever profits they eventually made. These shares were bought and sold in a market called a stock exchange. As individual ownership of businesses declined, and most came to be owned by thousands of shareholders, stock exchanges like those on New York's Wall Street became vital centers of the capitalist economy.

The Dark Side

For information on key people, see pages 59–60.

Many people, especially in North America and Europe, enjoyed capitalism's tremendous success. But by the end of the 19th century, doubts were beginning to grow. Many people had paid a high price for the wealth that had been created, and capitalism itself had moved far beyond the simplicity described by Adam Smith.

A different world

In the new industrial world, working conditions were usually unhealthy, the machinery was often dangerous, the air was full of poisons. For the first time in history, millions of people were working set hours under the constant supervision of others. Few of them had any say in what they were making, how quickly they worked, or what happened to the product after they made it. They had become just cogs in a machine.

Some owners and managers tried to improve conditions for their workers, and to treat them like fellow human beings, but under capitalism the need for **profits** always came first. If a capitalist business needed to cut its costs in order to compete, then lowering wages or laying off workers was often the best way to reduce them. The workers were cut off from the countryside and the ability to feed themselves. They were now completely dependent on their wages, and at the mercy of their employers.

Dark times

"It was a town of machinery and tall chimneys, out of which interminable serpents of smoke trailed themselves for ever and ever, and never got uncoiled. It had a black canal in it, and a river that ran purple with ill-smelling dye, and vast piles of buildings full of windows where there was a rattling and a trembling all day long, and where the piston of the steam-engine worked monotonously up and down like the head of an elephant in a state of melancholy madness."

(writer Charles Dickens describing fictional Coketown in *Hard Times*, his novel about the horrors of the Industrial Revolution)

Of course, if more members of a family worked, the family could make more money. In the early years of capitalism, women and children also worked long hours in terrible conditions since that was the only way they could find the means to live. The system thrived on their cheap labor, but great resentment also began to grow. Capitalism was producing wealth beyond the wildest dreams of earlier centuries, but it was ending up in far fewer pockets than seemed fair. Too many people were living lives plagued by insecurity, poverty, and poor health.

This photograph was taken in a cotton mill in Georgia early in the 20th century. These two young boys worked long hours for low pay.

The market grows less free

During the second half of the 19th century, many working people began supporting measures to reform capitalism. They demanded improved working conditions, a larger share of the profits, and better legal rights. They argued that governments should give **benefits** to those who were unable to work, either because they were too old or because there were not enough jobs to go around.

They formed **trade unions** to push their demands on employers, and also formed **socialist** political parties to push their arguments on governments. In the period at the end of the 19th and beginning of the 20th centuries, this pressure began to pay off. Retirement pensions and **unemployment benefits** were both introduced in many of the richer countries.

This is a famous 19th-century drawing of an overcrowded and polluted industrial landscape. In fact, at this time most country dwellings, although more picturesque, were no healthier.

Pressure from workers pushed wages higher than in an entirely free market, and employers found that they could raise their prices, too. During the second half of the 19th century, the size of businesses increased, leaving fewer and fewer in each sector of the market. As a result, there was less real competition.

When only three blanket manufacturers were left in the market, for example, it was relatively easy for their bosses to reach a secret agreement on what price they would all charge. There were attempts to keep companies from working together in such a way—the U.S. **anti-trust laws** of the 1890s, for example—but they were largely ineffective.

Trade between nations was also taking place in an increasingly unfree market. The United Kingdom, as the capitalist world leader for most of the 19th century, naturally wanted to promote free trade between nations.

Factory work was often extremely boring. These women workers in a factory in Liverpool, England, in the 1920s are frosting cookies with colored sugar.

The United Kingdom's products were cheaper and better, and sold well abroad. For those nations struggling to catch up, however, the opposite was true. In order to protect their own industries while they grew, these nations adopted a protectionist policy. This not only stifled free trade but also helped to poison international relations.

By 1900, the free market imagined by Adam Smith had all but disappeared, and capitalism was beginning to encounter serious problems. It was still showing an amazing ability to create wealth, but it was now also demonstrating a tendency to encourage serious conflicts, both within and between nations.

Free trade and protectionism

In a free market the most efficient businesses prosper and the least efficient usually fail. In international terms, this might mean that country A's efficient steel industry would prosper and country B's inefficient one would fail, leaving steel consumers in country B to buy their steel from country A. The government of country A would be happy about this; its workers would be fully employed and its steel exports would be earning the country money. Where steel was concerned, country A would be all in favor of a free international market, or free trade.

The government of country B would not be happy. All its steel workers would be unemployed and it would be paying for foreign steel. It would probably prefer to protect its own steel industry by charging a fee, or **tariff**, on each ton of steel that country A tried to bring in. This would make country A's steel more expensive than it really was in country B, and let country B's industry compete in its own market. The use of such tariffs to protect home industries is called protectionism.

The Crises of Capitalism

World War I threw the world economy off balance. Some countries, such as the United Kingdom, France, and Germany, were exhausted by the financial cost of fighting the war, while others, such as the United States and Japan, prospered. The decision by the victorious powers to make Germany pay **reparations** in punishment for starting the war made matters worse, and by the early 1920s the west European economies were in deep trouble. The leadership of the world economy had passed from the United States to the United Kingdom. The United States firmly believed that capitalism was capable of sorting itself out without interference from the politicians.

The Great Depression

The United States wrong. Between 1925 and 1928 the developed economies grew. However, there were already signs of a slowdown in the United States when the **Great Crash** of the U.S. stock market in October 1929 triggered a collapse in the U.S. economy. This led in turn to a shrinking of the entire world economy, which became known as the **Great Depression.** In the years that followed, thousands of companies around the world went bankrupt, millions of workers became unemployed, and trade collapsed. It seemed as if capitalism's famous growth machine had shifted into reverse. Instead of success creating success, failure had bred failure.

Capitalism no longer looked like a system that worked, and it even began to look like one that was morally wrong. How, people asked, could one justify pouring out milk that hungry people needed, simply because they had no money to pay for it? Many critics pointed to the communist and **fascist** countries, which seemed—wrongly, as it later turned out—to be coping better with the Great Depression than capitalist countries were.

Post-war blues

"It is not intelligent. It is not beautiful. It is not just. It is not virtuous. And it doesn't deliver the goods."

(British economist John Maynard Keynes describing international capitalism in the aftermath of World War I)

Regulating capitalism

Faced with the Great Depression, the governments of the leading democratic countries—the United States, United Kingdom, France—waited in vain for capitalism to straighten itself out. Only when this did not happen did they listen to those who said that the governments themselves should straighten it out.

For information on key people, see pages 59–60.

A line of unemployed men in San Francisco during the Great Depression.

The best known of capitalism's critics was the UK economist, John Maynard Keynes. He had long argued that the perfect capitalism of the free market described by Adam Smith no longer existed. Businesses and trade unions had been able to keep prices and wages high.

This kept the market from working freely, and made it impossible for capitalism to regulate itself. Capitalism was like a boat with a broken rudder. It could still travel at speed, but it needed help steering a straight course.

The British economist John Maynard Keynes (1883–1946) was one of the first people to argue that capitalism needed to be regulated.

Only governments could provide that help. If they spent money when the economy was doing badly—as it was in the Great Depression—then that would encourage growth. At other times, when the economy was doing too well, and threatening to grow too fast, governments could raise **taxes** and **interest rates** to slow growth down. In such ways capitalism could be made more predictable, more reliable.

The first government to test Keynes's theory was the U.S. administration headed by President Roosevelt. The theory worked. Spending programs, known as the New Deal, kick-started the U.S. economy back into motion and slowly but surely put the United States back to work. World War II finally ended unemployment, although by then most capitalist states had adopted Keynes' ideas. Once the war was over, most governments, especially in Europe, were careful to manage and regulate their national economies. In Europe, many large private businesses—such as the railroads in the United Kingdom—were taken into **public ownership** and run by the government.

The New Deal

The New Deal was the name given to the 1933–1937 attempt by the Roosevelt administration to overcome the Great Depression with a program of government spending. Millions of unemployed men and women were paid by the government to do a variety of tasks—building new houses and dams, fixing railroads, planting new forests, even picking up leaves. The money they were paid was spent on goods, which helped other businesses get back on their feet. Slowly the economy began to grow again.

In both the United States and Europe, large increases in government spending—which were usually paid for by government borrowing—were used to stimulate the economy. The result was a return to growth. Between 1950 and the early 1970s, the regulated capitalist economies—including a lively West Germany and Japan—boomed, their industrial outputs increasing four-fold. New industries, such as plastics and electronics grew rapidly, keeping unemployment low. In many countries, governments used high tax **revenues** to pay for increasing health and **welfare benefits**. The growth machine was back on track, and this time it seemed to have a more caring side. Capitalism had become welfare capitalism, a system that not only produced wealth but also took care of its people.

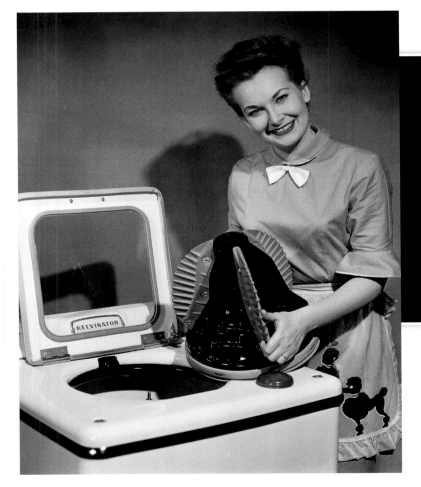

By the 1950s, the capitalist economies were booming and consumers had money to spend on new household goods, such as this washing machine.

A new crisis

The post-war boom lasted until the early 1970s, when most economies of the developed world found they were suffering from something Keynes had thought was impossible—a combination of high **inflation** and high unemployment. There was no obvious single cause for this state of affairs, and economists disagreed about how important the various causes were. Some singled out the rise in oil prices that followed an Arab–Israeli War in 1973. Some believed it was the result of the United States borrowing to pay for the Vietnam War (1963–1975). Others pointed to the high level of government spending, which was needed to pay for the welfare benefits now taken for granted.

During the 1970s, oil prices rose steeply and there were several scares about shortages in supplies. Service stations like this one in California were jammed with cars as people tried to stock up on gasoline.

Whatever the cause, capitalism once again seemed to be failing. Unemployment rose and goods became more expensive. The crisis was not as desperate as it had been in the 1930s, and this time around there were no obvious competitors to mount a challenge. Fascism was a disgraced memory, and it was becoming increasingly obvious that communism was unable to create the type of highly developed economy that existed under capitalism.

Deregulating capitalism

Capitalism's answer to the new crisis was to turn its back on Keynes. The influential economists of the 1970s, such as Milton Friedman and Friedrich von Hayek (both of whom won the Nobel Prize for economics in that decade), argued for a return to a purer, unregulated capitalism. They wanted governments to create the conditions for pure competition—such as by weakening the power of unions to keep wages higher—and then step back.

Versions of these theories were put into practice by the governments of Ronald Reagan in the United States and Margaret Thatcher in the United Kingdom. They put many state-owned companies back into private ownership (**privatization**), introduced laws to weaken the unions, and tried to cut government spending, especially on welfare. Their example was followed by governments around the world, although in continental Europe there was some resistance to the reduction of welfare benefits. By 1990, when communism suddenly collapsed in eastern Europe, capitalism was more than triumphant—it had recovered the dynamic image of the glory days of the 19th century. The result, predictably, was two-fold. The last decade of the 20th century was marked by rapid growth and an increase in inequality, both within and between nations.

The Politics of Capitalism

Capitalism is a type of economic system. As we have seen, it has profound social consequences. It has changed patterns of working and greatly altered the overall distribution of wealth. But what political consequences has it had? How has capitalism changed the way countries are governed?

Liberalism

Adam Smith believed that the free market worked best when left to itself. He considered any form of government intervention at best a necessary evil. He accepted that governments needed to provide facilities that the market would not—things such as schools, the armed forces, the legal system—but he insisted that its only other economic role was to remove any restrictions on the free working of the market. If the free market was like a river, then governments had to act like mechanical dredgers, making sure that the riverbed was clear of obstacles so that the water could flow.

This painting shows a mob burning down a farm in Kent, England, to protest the British Corn Laws, which kept the price of grain high and were eventually repealed in 1846.

This desire to liberalize, or free, the workings of the market was the driving power behind **liberalism**, the dominant political force of early 19th-century capitalism. Liberals wanted to help capitalism overcome obstacles, such as outdated restrictions on certain types of economic activity, or the continuing power of those who felt threatened by the rise of the new capitalist class.

In order to change such regulations, and to override the power of the traditional ruling classes, the new liberalizing capitalist class needed to promote and strengthen those **democratic** institutions that already existed in North America and Europe. In most cases they were only elected by a small, property-owning portion of the male population (no one else had the right to vote). These institutions could then be used to make life easier for capitalism.

Some of the liberal changes benefited everyone. The abolition of taxes on newspapers, for example, led to cheaper papers and a wider spread of information. This helped businessmen make profitable decisions, and increased the information available to ordinary citizens.

Other measures were of less benefit to the majority of the population. Giving money to the poor was discouraged, because it might encourage them not to work, and trade unions were outlawed because they increased the bargaining power of workers. The liberals of the time considered that both charity and collective bargaining interfered with the free working of the capitalist market.

Capitalism and slavery

The early 19th-century drive to abolish slavery, which was largely led by the liberal middle class, was a good example of how and why capitalism encouraged the spread of liberty. No doubt many individual capitalists objected to slavery on moral grounds, but from Adam Smith's point of view the principal objection to slavery was that it interfered with the free working of the labor market. Capitalism needed free workers, who could move from place to place and change jobs.

Socialism

As the 19th century unfolded, capitalism's ability to create wealth was matched by its tendency to divide up the wealth unequally. Those with capital to invest always did much better than those who only had their labor to sell. Some help was given by governments to those on the bottom rungs of the economic ladder—the employment of children under the age of nine, for example, was banned in the United Kingdom by the Factory Act of 1833. However, resentment continued to grow, and in the second half of the century it found political expression in the growth of trade unions and socialist parties.

The central argument of these groups was that capitalism, left to itself, caused too much misery to too many people. They agreed that capitalism was an efficient producer of wealth, but claimed that it was not able to make sure that everyone received a fair share. If capitalism itself could not do this, then governments had to. Socialists believed that governments had to intervene in the economy for the sake of the people as a whole.

There were several ways that governments could do this. They could pay social security benefits to people of retirement age, and they could pay unemployment benefits to those who could not find work. They could tax the rich more heavily and use the money from this to make life more comfortable for the poor. They could even take unprofitable industries, such as the railroads, into public ownership and use taxpayers' money to keep them afloat, thus safeguarding the jobs of those who worked in them. They could do some or all of these things, but each one of them amounted to intervention in the free working of the market.

The 20th century

The politics of capitalism in the 20th century revolved around the question: how much intervention should there be? A few extreme liberals still argued for the type of minimal intervention favored by Adam Smith, while 20th-century communists argued for maximum intervention, the ending of the free market, and almost complete government control over all economic activity. Most political debate, though, has been between those on the moderate **right**, who favor a little intervention, and those on the moderate **left**, who favor more intervention.

Those on the moderate right—which makes up a large portion of both major political parties in the United States—have usually argued that too much intervention threatens individual freedoms and makes capitalism less efficient. They claim that a free, efficient capitalism is in everyone's best interests because it produces more wealth to share, no matter how unfair the distribution. Those on the moderate left—liberals in the United States—have argued that more government intervention can compensate for capitalism's tendency to promote inequality. It can help to create a fairer, more democratic society. Such an outcome, they claim, is well worth any small losses in personal freedom or economic efficiency that might result.

A poster at Waterloo Station in London, announcing that Britain's railroads had been taken over by state ownership. This was one way in which a government could intervene in the economy to protect workers' jobs and public services.

Roughly speaking, the moderate left won this argument between the 1930s and the early 1970s. In both North America and Europe, government intervention in capitalist economies was far more widespread after the Great Depression than it had been before. But during the last quarter of the 20th century, this situation was reversed. The moderate right took control, and government intervention in most developed countries was reduced.

The very nature of capitalism—its ability to generate both wealth and unfairness—means that the argument between those who put wealth first and those who put fairness first will continue as long as capitalism itself.

For information on key people, see pages 59–60.

During the 1980s, President Ronald Reagan and British Prime Minister Margaret Thatcher both took steps to restrict the role of government in their countries' economies.

Capitalism and democracy

Some people have argued, and others have simply taken it for granted, that free market capitalism and democracy were made for each other. This is not true. Indeed, throughout capitalism's 19th-century golden age, the number of adults allowed to vote was strictly limited. **Universal suffrage** was only introduced in the richer countries in the 20th century, and it has still not been introduced in some countries, for example, Saudi Arabia which plays an important role in the world capitalist system.

Certain features of capitalism have favored democracy, especially in the developed countries. For capitalism to work, individuals must have economic freedom, and political freedom seems like the natural next step. However, other aspects of capitalism have worked against democracy. Wealthy industrialists, for example, have the power to influence governments more than poor individuals.

Capitalism and freedom

Capitalism and freedom are often grouped together, as if they are virtually the same thing. This is only partly true. Capitalism needs a free market—that is, one in which governments try not to interfere in the buying and selling of goods and services. It also relies on a spirit of free enterprise, on individual ambition and initiative. It requires what philosophers have called the "freedoms to"—such as to trade, or speak their mind—those freedoms that allow people to do what they individually wish to do within agreed rules of law.

Capitalism does not, however, need the full range of political freedoms that are generally enjoyed in early 21st-century North America and Europe. It has worked perfectly well in a variety of political environments—**colonial rule**, civil and military **dictatorship**, even communist dictatorships like present-day China—where political freedoms have been severely limited. Capitalism has also often failed to make room for what philosophers call the "freedoms from"—like freedom from hunger, unemployment, insecurity, and fear.

Communism: Enemy of Capitalism?

Capitalism faced two major challenges in the 20th century. The first of these came from within. It involved reforming and regulating itself to the point where it became acceptable to a large majority of the population. The second, the challenge of communism, came from outside. This second challenge was political, economic and, at times, even military.

Communism comes to power

Communism was a response to capitalism's failure in certain parts of the world. Nowhere were these failings more apparent than in Russia, where working conditions were dreadful, the gap between rich and poor was enormous, and much of industry's profit went into the hands of foreign capitalists rather than the workers. Unsurprisingly, it was here, in October 1917, that Vladimir Lenin led the world's first successful communist revolution. His supporters were delighted by his proposal to replace cruel capitalism with the fairer-sounding socialism.

Similar chains of events later took place in China and Cuba. Before their revolutions—in 1949 and 1959 respectively—both of these countries experienced many of capitalism's negative points, and only a few of its positive points. Cubans and Chinese were willing to try to create something different.

Abolishing capitalism

The Russian communists abolished capitalism. The private ownership of most property was brought to an end, leaving no basis for a competitive free market. All economic decisions—what to produce, where and how to produce it—were now taken by the visible hand of government, rather than what Adam Smith called the invisible hand of the free market. Government planners decided to invest in a new steel mill or a new dam because they thought the country needed such things, not because they expected to make a profit out of them. This, the communists claimed, was both more rational—it meant that only what was really needed got produced—and fairer. There were no capitalists at the top enjoying huge profits, no workers at the bottom slaving away for others' gain.

For information on key people, see pages 59–60.

There was some truth in this, but only some. It turned out that economic planning worked well only in the early stages of industrialization; once the economy grew more complicated, the visible hand of government direction proved much more clumsy and inefficient than the invisible hand of the market. It also turned out that, profits or no profits, those who ran the system still managed to enjoy an unfair share of what was produced. Communism was not much fairer than capitalism.

The message on this propaganda poster from the Russian Revolution reads: "You still haven't joined the Co-operative—sign up immediately!"

Finally, and perhaps most importantly of all, the lack of economic freedom went hand in hand with a lack of political freedom. Creativity was stifled, innovation discouraged, individual ambition and enthusiasm dulled. Communism lacked the very things that had turned capitalism into a growth machine.

During the final years of the communist Soviet Union, there were shortages of many goods. People often had to stand in line for hours just to buy food.

Lenin on capitalism

"Capitalists are no more capable of self-sacrifice than a man is capable of lifting himself up by his own bootstraps."

(Russian communist leader Vladimir Lenin, stating his belief that, under capitalism, the rich did not want to help the poor and the poor were unable to help themselves.)

Cold War

Communism's failings took a long time to become apparent. In the 1930s, when the leading capitalist countries were dragging along the bottom of the Great Depression, communist Russia seemed to be forging ahead with its ambitious **five-year plans.** The level of suffering in the West was well known, the much greater level of suffering in Russia hardly known at all. Russian military success in World War II and its amazing economic recovery that followed only heightened communism's reputation.

By 1950, however, the capitalist world had also recovered economically, and through the first 20 years of the **Cold War** (1948–1968) each of the two systems tried to prove that it was more efficient than the other. Capitalism and communism also competed for influence in the developing countries of Asia, Africa, and Latin America, where the capitalist world was at a definite disadvantage. For one thing, the capitalist countries— either as colonial powers or simple economic bullies—were considered responsible for the poverty that existed throughout the developing world. For another, communism seemed good at providing the type of basic economic development that many of the poorer countries so desperately needed. It had worked for Russia and China, so why not for other undeveloped countries?

Eventually, however, the failure of the communist countries to produce the wide range of goods that their people wanted, and which the advanced capitalist countries took for granted, resulted in the collapse of European communism and an end, in all but name, to communism in east Asia. By 1991, capitalism's triumph over its enemy was virtually complete.

The only sour note was the continuing poverty of many developing nations. In this area things did not seem to have changed at all: it was just such a stark contrast between rich and poor that had originally attracted so many in the developing world to communism in the early part of the 20th century.

Capitalism and the Poorer Countries

The enormous wealth that capitalism generated throughout the 19th and 20th centuries was not spread evenly across the globe. Some countries were much richer than others, and all countries had their rich and poor. As the 20th century ended, these gaps kept growing wider. Roughly a quarter of the world's people—most of them living in the world's poorest countries—had an income of less than $370 a year. For these people, capitalism was obviously not working very well.

Colonialism and after

Some people blamed this situation on colonialism, the rule of economically undeveloped countries by economically advanced countries. They claimed that European powers, such as the United Kingdom and

This painting shows British ships lining the docks at the port of Calcutta in India during the days of the British Empire.

France, which had ruled large areas of the world for several centuries, had held back the countries they had occupied. Rather than give or sell modern technology to these countries, and let them create their own industrial revolution, these colonial powers had used them as sources of raw materials and markets for their own industrial products. The United Kingdom, for example, had set their taxes and **tariffs** in such a way that, even in cotton-growing India, British-made textiles were able to undercut those produced locally.

However, colonialism's apologists pointed out that colonial powers also improved the basic facilities of the countries they occupied. They left them with better roads, railroads, ports, and fairer law and administration.

Most direct colonial rule came to an end during the second half of the 20th century, but those most critical of the rich countries' behavior in what became known as the third (or developing) world argue that little really changed. Countries gained political independence, but they were still economically dependent on the richer countries. The World Bank and International Monetary Fund were supposed to provide help, but they were effectively controlled by the United States and the old colonial powers.

Overseeing the international economy

There are three major international economic organizations. The International Bank for Reconstruction and Development (generally known as the World Bank) and the International Monetary Fund (IMF) were both formed in 1945 with the goal of encouraging world economic development. Both have loaned large amounts of money to developing countries, much of which they have been unable to repay. In the late 1990s, a worldwide campaign was launched to cancel many of the outstanding debts.

The World Trade Organization **(WTO)** was founded in 1995 as the successor to the General Agreement on Tariffs and Trade (GATT). Its main task is to regulate trade and, where possible, take away barriers to free trade. Since free trade tends to benefit the richer, more efficient producing countries, the WTO has also been subject to a campaign of protest.

According to capitalism's critics, people and businesses in the richer countries held on to most of the economic power. They decided where to invest their capital in new businesses and jobs. The poorer countries, like average workers in the United States in the early 19th century, had to accept whatever they were offered. They had little bargaining power of their own.

Capitalism's supporters had a more positive view of its record in the developing world. They pointed to the success of what were called the **Asian Tigers**—countries such as South Korea, Taiwan, Singapore, and Malaysia—that had managed to lift themselves out of poverty by stressing education and hard work, and by keeping wages low. These countries had successfully competed with the rich nations by doing exactly what Adam Smith would have recommended. They had made products the richer nations wanted, such as electronic goods, cheaper and more efficiently than the richer nations could make themselves.

This assembly plant in Durban, South Africa is owned by the Japanese company, Toyota. Multinational corporations like Toyota provide jobs for people in many of the world's poorer countries.

Opting out

The most important change to affect the international economy over the last quarter century has been the growing power of **multinational corporations**. These businesses, which conduct operations all around the world, often have higher incomes and expenditures than national governments. Their supporters claim that they bring new technology, new management methods, and new jobs to the poorer countries, and should therefore be welcomed. Their critics argue that the jobs are few, that major decisions are all made at corporate headquarters in the rich countries, and that most of the profits are sent home to the rich countries. These critics claim that the multinational corporations, far from developing the poorer countries, use them as a source of cheap labor.

In order to protect themselves from the overwhelming power of foreign economic interests, some of the poorer countries have tried to opt out of the world capitalist system. In the early 1960s, for example, Cuba joined the communist world when its revolutionary leaders realized that staying in the capitalist system would mean domination by its neighbor, the United States. In Tanzania, President Julius Nyerere tried to introduce a form of African socialism in semi-isolation from the capitalist world. In the early years of the 21st century, President Hugo Chavez of oil-rich Venezuela turned his back on U.S.-style capitalism and decided to base his country on socialist principles.

Anti-capitalists have met with some success. Cuba's system of health care, for example, was considered the best in Latin America. Generally speaking, however, the attempts made by small countries to step outside the capitalist system were a failure. Capitalism overwhelmed them: its economic success proved impossible to ignore, and its economic (and sometimes its military) power impossible to resist.

Extending welfare capitalism?

Over the last hundred years, the whole world has learned what North America and Europe learned in the 19th century, that capitalism creates both wealth and inequality. The North American and European answer was to regulate and reform capitalism, to the point where it offered something even to those at the bottom of the economic ladder. If the widening gap between rich and poor countries is to be narrowed, it seems likely that something similar must be introduced at the international level. How this can be achieved, when there is no prospect of meaningful international government, is one of the most important questions facing people and politicians in the 21st century.

These poverty-stricken Egyptian women and children survive by rummaging through a dump in search of food and things to sell. Critics of multinational corporations claim that they often do not bring wealth to the poorer countries where their factories are based.

Capitalism and the Environment

If capitalism did manage to raise the economic level of the world's poorer countries to that enjoyed today by the richer countries, it would, unfortunately, find itself with another problem. Experts have estimated that this level of economic growth would need a five-fold increase in world energy consumption, at a time when current levels are already creating major problems for the environment.

Dark beginnings

As early as 1804, the British writer William Blake published a poem contrasting the dark, satanic (hell-like) mills of the Industrial Revolution with the green and pleasant land that they were replacing. As the century unfolded, things only changed for the worse. Each year, thousands of new factories in North America and western Europe coughed coal smoke and unhealthy gases into the air, darkening the daytime sky over rapidly growing towns.

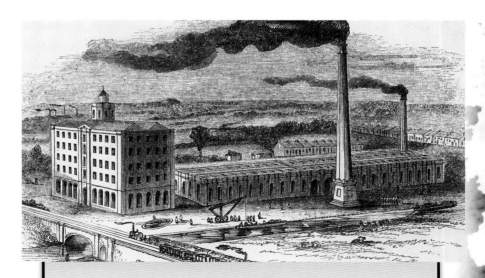

This is a newly built metal works in Somerset, England, 1840. The writer William Blake was critical of the way that factories like this spoiled the English countryside.

Most governments did not make any attempts to limit either this polluting of the atmosphere, or the poisoning of the rivers with industrial waste. For well over a century, capitalist industry was allowed to take its profits without cleaning up after itself.

Things began to change around the middle of the 20th century. The areas affected by industrial pollution had slowly grown, and now included large parts of the most developed countries. London, for example, experienced serious smogs (industrial fogs) in the early 1950s. One of these is believed to have killed several hundred people. Both in London and elsewhere, a serious effort was made to clean up industry. This was made easier by the fact that coal-fired industries were, in many cases, already giving way to alternatives that caused less pollution.

Environmental disaster?

We now know that smoke and garbage—the visible refuse from capitalist enterprises—are a far less serious threat to the planet than the invisible gases, such as carbon dioxide, that pour into the atmosphere and cause **global warming.** In 2006, it was shown that since the dawn of the modern capitalist era in the late 18th century, the planet's average temperature has risen by over 1 °F (0.5 °C). Far more alarming, this increase was accelerating rapidly, so that some people were predicting an overall increase of perhaps 10 °F (5 °C) by the end of the 21st century. The effects of such a change are impossible to predict accurately, but they certainly include massive flooding of all the world's low-lying areas, crop failure, and famine. These would inevitably trigger political turmoil and human disasters on an unimaginable scale. In other words, it looks as if the human race might reap a tragic harvest from the capitalist seeds it has sown.

Capitalist seeds? What does global warming have to do with capitalism? Capitalism works by making profit; this profit is the difference between the cost of manufacturing something and the price received for selling it. In other words, capitalism depends on manufacturing, which in turn requires energy. Many believe this consumption of energy, largely in the form of fossil fuels such as coal and oil, has produced the large expansion of greenhouse gases that is causing our world to heat up. Thus capitalism and the industrialization it requires may be responsible for the most serious crisis ever to face the human race.

The price of capitalism? Some environmental scientists believe that pollution like this from a Canadian paper mill has already permanently changed the Earth's climate, making life harder for millions of people.

Some argue that capitalism is also responsible for the world's slow reaction to the problem of environmental pollution. It is said that large and extremely powerful companies, whose profits dwarf the income of many small and medium-sized countries, put pressure on governments—particularly that of the United States—not to take action on pollution. They fear that anti-pollution measures would reduce their profits. Governments are tempted to go along with this, too, because a large part of their revenue comes from the taxes collected from company profits.

Capitalism's problem?

Despite the arguments put forward in the last paragraph, there are those who say that environmental damage is caused by industrialization, not capitalism. They point out, quite correctly, that communist states—the USSR before 1990 and modern-day China—have terrible records on industrial pollution. By opening hundreds of new coal-fired power stations every year, for example, in the early part of the 21st century China was increasing its output of greenhouse gases despite their effect on the environment.

In response to this, it may be pointed out that Russia and China's industrialization was begun by capitalists and continued by the communists in an effort to show that communism was just as effective at producing wealth as capitalism. Indeed, modern-day China, while keeping its communist politics, has wholeheartedly adopted capitalist economics. Many believe there is no escaping it: capitalism lies behind our escalating environmental problems.

Too many cars—a traffic jam in Boston contributes to the global warming problem.

Capitalism's solutions?

The outlook is by no means all gloomy, however. Capitalism's great strengths are those of human beings in general: enormous energy, enterprise, and adaptability. It is quite reasonable to expect, therefore, that just as capitalism has produced the problem of climate change, so it will be able to solve it. As long as there are profits to be made, capitalists will find a way of doing something.

A start has already been made. Products, such as cars, are already advertised as being more environmentally friendly than others. Multinational oil companies, such as BP, are spending billions on research into alternative energy sources such as wind and wave power. Just as capitalists, under government direction, made profits out of solving the problems of slums and disease caused by the Industrial Revolution, so they have begun to tackle the latest crisis. After all, it is not in anyone's interest, least of all the capitalists, to destroy the planet on which they prosper.

Toll roads

Toll roads are a good example of how, under capitalism, polluters can be made to pay for the pollution they cause. If car owners are charged for using city streets, they will use their cars less, which will lower the level of exhaust emissions. When they do choose to pay the charges and use their cars, the money collected can be used to improve public transportation systems. Once public transportation is improved, more people will choose to use it, and this will lessen pollution even more. And in the meantime, the high cost of using cars that pollute will have created a new and growing market for cars that do not.

Globalization

By the final decade of the 20th century, capitalism had taken over the entire international economy. The end of communism in Europe and the opening up of communist China to capitalist enterprise were two reasons for this. Others included advances in telecommunications and computing, and the growth of multinational corporations. This whole process—the capitalist takeover—is known as globalization.

In the 1980s and 1990s, many restrictions on international trade were removed, and multinational corporations were able to start moving their capital around the world in search of the best deals. Not surprisingly, they often chose to set up their operations in poorer countries, such as Mexico or Indonesia, where cheaper labor (workers who cost less) reduced the cost of production. It also often made sense for them to get local businesses to do the manufacturing. That way, the corporation did not have to pay the local workers unemployment or health benefits.

Workers in Austin, Texas, demonstrate against the North American Free Trade Association in November 1993. Many were afraid that companies would move their operations to Mexico, where wages were lower.

Consequences for the richer countries

Capitalism's globalization had important consequences for all countries. Most developed states grew richer from the worldwide growth of the 1990s. At the same time, in the less flexible capitalist states, such as France, a number of people lost their jobs as multinational corporations moved their operations abroad in search of cheaper labor. Some advanced capitalist countries, notably the United States and the United Kingdom, managed to avoid rising unemployment by keeping their labor markets free and open. However, this often meant low wages and long hours for the less well off—but that was the capitalist system.

The richer countries were also facing competition from newly developing countries, such as the Asian Tigers and China, which had lower wages and spent less on welfare. Sometimes, as when the European Union found its shoe industry was being undermined by millions of pairs of cheap shoes from China in 2004–2005, there was talk of turning away from the capitalist free market and protecting European industries with new tariffs. In order to compete successfully with these new rivals, the richer countries had to cut back the benefits they paid out to their own people. The poorest got less help than before, which also increased inequality.

The rise of international corporations and banks that held such enormous power also posed a threat to national governments. They could no longer feel in complete control of their own countries. This is what one French government discovered in the early 1980s, when it tried to introduce a socialist program. International business began withdrawing capital from France, which reduced the value of the French currency. The government was forced to reconsider its program.

Keeping down costs

In Bob Dylan's song "North Country Blues" (1963), he tells the story of how a North American mine has been forced to close by foreign competition. The South American mine is more competitive because the local workers are prepared to work for almost nothing.

The French government, as in most capitalist democracies, had been freely elected by its people. Yet its wishes were simply overridden by the interests of an international business community that no one had elected. As an increasing number of experts were pointing out, globalization clearly had serious consequences for democracy.

Consequences for the poorer countries

If the governments of the rich countries could be frightened by the new powers of the international economy, then what hope did the governments of the poor countries have? Their bargaining power was weaker than ever, and in order to create jobs they had to offer huge incentives (rewards), such as low taxes, to multinationals thinking of setting up a local branch of their business. In some cases, health and safety regulations were ignored, bribes offered and taken, and protesters quickly jailed. As a result, many new factories in the poor countries were very similar to those of the United States at the start of the Industrial Revolution and early Victorian England, full of very young employees working long hours for very low pay.

This was capitalism's dark side in the early 21st century. In factories scattered around the world's poorest countries, young girls spent 14-hour work days making famous brand name goods for the type of wages that just barely covered their food and a room in a boarding house. The tennis shoes and clothes they made were sold by the local company to brand name companies in the West. These companies spent more on advertising their brand names than they had on the actual goods, and reaped enormous profits in return. On the other hand, it may be argued that although multinationals' wages were poor and working conditions bad, at least their employees in developing countries had jobs. In previous centuries, the poorest simply starved to death or died of disease through malnutrition. Capitalism has raised everyone's expectations.

Consequences for everyone

Globalization had other results for the world as a whole. One was a greater homogeneity, or sameness, in the products that were bought and sold around the world. More and more, we find the same fast foods, clothes brands, music, and fashions in the farthest corners of the globe.

The success of Western capitalism at selling Western products is resulting in increased uniformity. Today, except in the very poorest places, the clothes worn by a crowd of people look pretty much the same all over the world. Meals are similar, too, as are cars and other products. Some older people are worried by this trend, but the young seem to like it. Most of the world's conflicts have been caused by cultural, political, economic, and religious differences, they point out, so anything that brings people closer together should be welcomed.

The women in this factory in Zhongshan, China are making brand-name tennis shoes for the Western market. Their low wages, while good by Chinese standards, allow their products to be sold at a substantial profit in the West.

Different country, same burgers: a McDonald's restaurant in Beijing, China. Traditionalists dislike this aspect of globalization, but it may be defended as helping to create the feeling of a more united global village.

A less welcome consequence of a globalized economy is insecurity. When work can be easily moved from country to country, few jobs are safe. Moreover, because national economies are so interlinked, bad news for one can sometimes easily become bad news for all. An event such as the terrorist attack on the World Trade Center in New York City on September 11, 2001, had adverse economic consequences for almost every family on Earth.

A brighter outlook?

Capitalism's supporters would argue that for all its problems, and for all its unfairness, it has raised the living standards of almost every community on Earth over the last century. Its greatest achievement has been to harness human ambition, ingenuity, and aggression into ways that benefit all, creating new ways of looking at the world.

Furthermore, capitalism also manages to find solutions to many of the problems it creates. Its profits paid to replace the substandard housing of the early Industrial Revolution; it created the Internet, a force for global democracy that counteracts the anti-democratic power of multinationals; and it is working on ways to tackle the climate change that its enterprise has triggered.

Whatever fears people might have about globalization and the power of multinational corporations, it is worth remembering the important lessons of history. Whenever capitalism has appeared to be acting against the best interests of the populations it claims to be serving, they have taken steps to tame it. Unrestricted free enterprise was curbed by laws banning monopolies, protecting working conditions and even, as in Russia and China, by anti-capitalist revolutions. More recently, in response to public pressure, governments have forced capitalist enterprises to clean up their acts and become more environmentally friendly. To date, therefore, capitalism has been humankind's servant, not its master—as long as we keep it this way, we have nothing to fear.

So, What Is Capitalism?

Capitalism is an economic system in which private individuals (or groups) use private capital (money or other forms of wealth, such as machinery) and labor to produce goods and services. These can be sold at a profit in a competitive market that is free and open to everyone. As a form of economic transaction, capitalism goes back to the first traders. As a dominant force in any society, it perhaps goes back to western Europe in the late 17th century. During that century and the next, it slowly tightened its hold on the economies of North America and western Europe, and over the last hundred years it has effectively conquered the globe.

Until the late 1980s, the Pudong district of Shanghai, China, was mostly farmland. Today, thanks to the Chinese government's acceptance of capitalist economics, it has been transformed into a stunning new city.

History and politics

The central fact of capitalism is that, left to itself, it tends to generate both wealth and inequality. Everyone on Earth has benefited, at least to some degree, from the generation of wealth, but the generation of inequality at the same time has led to many social and political crises.

The history of capitalism is an endless search for compromise, between allowing it to create wealth and controlling its crueler side with government regulations and restrictions. Without such government intervention, those who work for pay, supplying the labor that turns capital into goods and services, have usually been given an unsatisfactory share of the wealth that could not have been generated without their labor.

This was particularly obvious during the Great Depression. Afterward, government intervention in the capitalist economies was at its height. In the late 1970s, a new phase in capitalist history began, with governments of almost all persuasions relaxing their efforts to regulate the free market. This resulted in tremendous growth worldwide, but also in increased pollution and the growth of gigantically powerful multinational corporations. Some of these, such as the American Enron Corporation, were shown to be little more than gigantic swindles. By the early 21st century, therefore, the pendulum was beginning to swing back the other way, as governments started to regulate capitalism more closely again.

Generally speaking, socialist-inclined governments of the left have favored intervention to regulate capitalism, while those of the right have been happier for it to have free rein. However, a capitalist system can operate under any government that allows economic freedom to flourish. It is harder to make this work in a situation where there is no political freedom, but it is quite possible. This has been shown by many military governments over the last few decades. Capitalism tends to favor political freedom, but it can survive without it.

The only serious attempt to abolish capitalism took place in Soviet Russia and the states it dominated in eastern Europe after World War II, in China after 1949, and in North Korea, Cuba, Vietnam, and other communist states around the world.

Some of capitalism's faults were dealt with—guaranteeing every citizen a job, for example, banished the fear of unemployment—but overall the communist experiment was a failure. The replacement of private property and the free market with government planning lessened economic efficiency and took away people's freedoms.

Protests and prospects

Communism's collapse at the end of the 1980s left capitalism triumphant, but the applause did not last for long. In the newly capitalist states, the gap between rich and poor widened, leading to social problems such as rising crime. Environmental damage increased, too. Globalization was not only making these problems worse, but also creating new ones for democracy in the richer countries. Through the 1990s, a campaign of protest gathered momentum as people, angered by exploitation in the poorer countries, or worried about threats to democracy and the environment, came together in a loose alliance against capitalism. These protests continued into the new century. A meeting of the leaders of the world's leading industrial nations, such as at Gleneagles, Scotland in 2005, inevitably produced an enormous wave of protest.

Anti-globalization protesters wave banners in Annemasse, France in 2003. The protest was targeted at the G8 summit taking place in nearby Evian, France.

Many believe that all these issues have a common thread—capitalism's basic heartlessness. They feel, in the words of one famous phrase, that capitalism "knows the price of everything and the real value of nothing." Most accept that capitalism remains the most efficient generator of wealth, but they point out that the system itself has no interest in helping the less fortunate. Individual capitalists may have such an interest, but it is the desire for profits, and not the desire to help others, that makes the whole system work.

Since capitalism cannot supply its own conscience, society must provide one for it. In the West, religion used to supply this conscience but today, especially outside of the United States, its influence has declined sharply. In Muslim states it remains strong, however. One explanation for the Islamic terrorists' hatred of the West is what they see as its crude, capitalist materialism, its pursuit of worldly treasure at the expense of holier virtues. Socialism has tried to give capitalism a conscience, pushing for more equality as capitalism pushes for less, but it has been tarnished by the record of its more extreme cousin, communism. It remains to be seen where competitive, individualistic capitalism will find the conscience it will certainly need to cope with the challenges of the 21st century.

Contrasting views on capitalism

Capitalism has always provoked controversy and strong opinions. Sylvia Pankhurst, the British lobbyist for the right of women to vote, vowed to "fight capitalism even if it kills me." She felt that it was wrong that some people should be comfortable and well-fed while others are starving. By contrast, the British Prime Minister Winston Churchill remarked that only socialists thought it was wrong to make a profit—the real crime was to make a loss. In the United States, President Eisenhower spoke admiringly of "the creative magic of free labor and capital," but his fellow American, the African-American leader Malcolm X, was not convinced. "Show me a capitalist," he said, "I'll show you a bloodsucker."

Timeline

1492	Columbus sails to the Americas
1500–1800	Age of commercial capitalism
early 1500s	Birth of Protestantism
mid-1700s	Beginning of Industrial Revolution in the United Kingdom
1764	James Hargreaves invents spinning-jenny textile machine
1767	Richard Arkwright invents water frame textile machine Adam Smith's *An Inquiry into the Nature and Causes of the Wealth of Nations* is published
1832	Reform Act increases the number of those allowed to vote in United Kingdom
1833	First Factory Act to regulate working conditions is introduced in United Kingdom
1848	Karl Marx and Friedrich Engels's *Communist Manifesto* is published
1851	The Great Exhibition is held in London
1860s	Worldwide growth of socialist parties
1867	First volume of Karl Marx's *Capital* (*Das Kapital*) published
1870–1914	United States and Germany overtake United Kingdom in industrial production
1890	Introduction of anti-trust laws in United States (Sherman Act)
1908	Introduction of Ford Model T, the first mass-produced car
1914–18	World War I
1917	The first **communist** revolution takes place in Russia
1918–19	Treaty of Versailles signed in Paris
1928	Soviet leadership introduces overall economy planning
1929	Great Crash on New York Stock Exchange (October)
1929–33	The worst years of the Great Depression
1933	President F. D. Roosevelt introduces first New Deal measures
1936	J. M. Keynes's *General Theory of Unemployment, Interest and Money* published
1939–45	World War II

1947	Cold War begins. United Kingdom gives independence to India (beginning of European decolonization)
1948	General Agreement on Tariffs and Trade (GATT) formed
1949	Founding of the Chinese People's Republic
1950–75	Capitalist economies boom in North America, western Europe and Japan
1957	European Economic Community (EEC) founded
1959	Cuban revolution
1961	Julius Nyerere becomes leader of Tanganyika (later renamed Tanzania)
1963–75	U.S. involvement in Vietnam War
1968	Spring of anti-capitalist protests in France
1973	Sharp rise in price of oil leads to a slowdown in capitalist economies
1974	Friedrich von Hayek wins Nobel Prize for Economics
1976	Milton Friedman wins Nobel Prize for Economics
1978	Deng Xiaoping introduces market reforms in communist China
1979–90	Margaret Thatcher is prime minister of United Kingdom
1981–89	Ronald Reagan is president of United States
1989–91	The end of communism in Europe
1992	European Economic Community (EEC) becomes European Union (EU)
1993	United States, Canada, and Mexico form North American Free Trade Agreement (NAFTA)
1995	World Trade Organization (WTO) is set up as successor to GATT
1997	Kyoto Agreement to control emissions that cause global warming. Economic slowdown begins in Asian Tiger economies
1999	Major anti-capitalist protest in Seattle
2001	Terrorist attack on New York and Washington, D.C.
2004	China signs an agreement with neighbors to create the world's largest free-trade area
2006	Meeting in Nairobi, Kenya, a United Nations conference agrees on further steps to combat global warming

Further Information

Further reading

Dickens, Charles. *Hard Times.* New York: Penguin, 2007.

Downing, David. *The Great Depression.* Chicago: Heinemann Library, 2001.

Forte, Imogene, and Marjorie Frank. *Global Studies*. Nashville, Tenn.: Incentive Publications, 2002.

Grant, R.G. *Capitalism.* New York: Raintree Steck-Vaughn, 2002.

Ritchie, Nigel. *Communism*. New York: Raintree Steck-Vaughn, 2001.

Ross, Stewart. *The Collapse of Communism.* Chicago: Heinemann Library, 2004.

Ross, Stewart. *The Industrial Revolution.* Danbury, Conn.: Franklin Watts, 2001.

Stein, Paul. *Global Warming: A Threat to Our Future*. New York: Rosen Publishing Group, 2001.

Steinbeck, John. *The Grapes of Wrath.* New York: Penguin, 2002.

Taylor, David. *The Cold War.* Chicago: Heinemann Library, 2001.

Websites

www.capitalism.org

www.greenpeace.org

www.imf.org

www.newdeal.feri.org

www.pbs.org/wgbh/amex/dustbowl/peopleevents/

www.theworldbank.org

www.wsu.edu/ ~ dee/glossary/capital.htm

www.wto.org

Key Figures in the History of Capitalism

Henry Ford (1863–1947) was the American engineer who founded the Ford Motor Company in Detroit in 1899. Nine years later he was the first manufacturer to introduce assembly-line production, for his famous Model T.

Milton Friedman (1912–2006) was professor of economic science at the University of Chicago from 1946 to 1983. He championed the free market, saying that government intervention in the economy should only be allowed to control inflation by limiting the amount of money in circulation. Like von Hayek, he found his ideas growing in popularity after the economic crises of the 1970s. Friedman won the Nobel Prize for Economics in 1976. He served as a policy adviser during Ronald Reagan's two terms as president (1981–1989).

Friedrich von Hayek (1899–1992), influential Austrian economist and political scientist. He held important academic posts in London (1931–50) and Chicago (1950–1962). In his most famous book, *The Road to Serfdom* (1944), he defended liberalism and the free market capitalism at a time when government intervention in the economy (Keynesianism) was more popular. After the crisis of the capitalist economies in the mid-1970s, many turned to his ideas, and in 1974 he shared the Nobel Prize for Economics.

John Maynard Keynes (1883–1946) was a UK economist who served as an adviser to the government in both World Wars. He criticized the Treaty of Versailles, correctly predicting that the decision to make Germany pay **reparations** would be disastrous for the whole international economy. Throughout the 1920s and 1930s, he argued for increased government intervention to spur economies on and reduce unemployment. His ideas helped influence President Roosevelt to introduce the New Deal.

Vladimir Ilyich Lenin (1870–1924) was the leader of the first communist revolution, the second Russian Revolution of 1917. Once in power he took the first steps in the abolition of capitalism in what became the Soviet Union. He vastly reduced private property rights and the operations of a free market.

Karl Marx (1818–1883) was the German **philosopher**, economist, and political scientist whose theories of social development helped inspire both socialism and communism. His most important work was *Capital* (*Das Kapital*), which both examined capitalism in detail and predicted its inevitable downfall.

Ronald Reagan (1911–2004) was a Hollywood actor who turned to politics. First he became governor of California and then president (1981–1989). He pursued right-wing policies, cutting taxes (particularly on business and the rich) and reducing government spending on provision of welfare benefits.

Franklin Delano Roosevelt (1882–1945) was elected president at the height of the Great Depression. His administration introduced the New Deal, a series of policies that involved spending government money to boost the economy and get people back to work.

Adam Smith (1723–1790), a Scottish economist and philosopher, is considered by many to be the founder of modern economics. He was the first to champion the emerging system of free market capitalism, and his book, *An Inquiry into the Nature and Causes of the Wealth of Nations* (1876), is still important.

Margaret Thatcher (1925–) took over as leader of the UK Conservative Party in 1975, and four years later became the first UK woman prime minister (1979–1990). Her government, the most right-wing the UK had seen in 50 years, championed free market capitalism and tried to reduce government intervention in the economy. The power of the trade unions was lessened, and publicly owned industries were returned to private ownership.

Glossary

anti-trust law law intended to keep companies from joining together in trusts to make private agreements to fix prices at a higher level than a free market would allow

aristocracy those who have inherited membership of the ruling elite by birth

Asian Tigers countries in the Far East and Southeast Asia that experienced rapid economic growth in the late 1990s

benefit payment made by a government to those who, for various reasons, are unable to work

capital money or other forms of wealth (such as land or machinery) that can be used to create goods or services

Cold War name given to the hostility that existed between the free enterprise capitalist and communist worlds between 1947 and the late 1980s

colonialism rule of economically undeveloped countries by economically advanced countries.

communism originally an extreme form of socialism, in which property is owned communally (in common) rather than individually. The term communism later became associated with the dictatorial state and system of economic planning that was created in the Soviet Union during the 1920s and 1930s.

democracy political system in which governments are regularly elected by the majority of the people, or a country in which this system exists

democratic reflecting the wishes of all those involved, often through voting

dictatorship government by an individual or a small group in which the majority of people have no say

Enlightenment period of the 18th century in which many European philosophers put more importance on reason and individualism than on tradition

exploitation taking advantage of, using selfishly or unfairly

fascism dictatorial system of government originating in Italy, which was later known for its aggressive nationalism. Nazism was one type of fascism.

fixed capital capital used to turn working capital into products; for example, the machinery used to make goods

five-year plan in communist countries, a plan of all intended economic activity over a five-year period

free market market that government does not regulate, or only regulates a little

global warming the gradual warming of the Earth's

atmosphere, which is mostly caused by rising levels of carbon dioxide gas

Great Crash sudden collapse of stock values on the New York Stock Exchange in October 1929, which helped to trigger the Great Depression

Great Depression period of great economic hardship that began around 1929, peaked around 1933, and lasted for most of the following decade. Most countries of the world were affected

Industrial Revolution change from a primarily agricultural economy to one based on large-scale production in factories that began in England in the 18th century

inflation increase in prices or increase in the supply of money (which leads to an increase in prices)

interest payments money repaid at regular intervals on a loan

interest rates when a loan is repaid, the extra amount charged for being allowed to take the loan

investment putting money into a project to make a profit

left(-wing) in politics, usually associated with policies that place the needs of the whole community (everyone) above the short-term needs of the individual

liberalism in the 19th century, a belief in the free market, free trade, and the removal of obstacles to either

multinational corporation large business that operates in several countries

philosopher someone who thinks, and often writes, about the bigger questions of human life

privatization returning publicly owned companies to private ownership

profit the difference between what is paid out and what comes back, when the latter is more than the former. For example, if an orange is bought for ten cents and sold for fifteen, then the seller makes a profit of five cents $(15-10 = 5)$.

Protestantism name given to the form of Christianity that split off from the Western Catholic church in the 16th-century Reformation

public ownership ownership by the people as whole, as represented by the government

Reformation 16th-century movement for reform in the Christian church that resulted in the split between Catholicism and Protestantism

reparations payments to make amends for war damage

revenue in a business or country, the money coming in

right(-wing) in politics, usually used to describe people and policies that favor individual interests over those of the community

self-regulating able to adapt to change without outside interference

stock certificate that people buy, which represents a piece of a business entitling the holders to a share of the profits

socialism set of political ideas that puts more stress on the needs of the community as a whole and less on the short-term wants or needs of the individual

tariff charge for bringing goods across international borders

taxes money paid to governments

tax incentive reduction of the money demanded by governments from businesses, with the intention of encouraging the business to move to a particular area

trade union organization formed to protect and advance the pay and conditions of workers

unemployment benefit money paid out on a regular basis by the government to the unemployed

universal suffrage all adults having the right to vote

welfare benefits money or services given to those who, through no fault of their own, are unable to support themselves fully

working capital capital used up in the creation of products, such as raw materials

World Trade Organization (WTO) international body founded in 1995 to regulate international economic activity

Index

First Facts™

The Solar System

Mercury

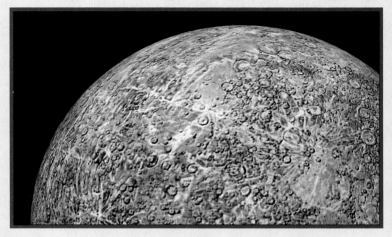

by Adele Richardson

Consultant:
Stephen J. Kortenkamp, PhD
Research Scientist
Planetary Science Institute, Tucson, Arizona

Capstone press
Mankato, Minnesota

First Facts is published by Capstone Press,
151 Good Counsel Drive, P.O. Box 669, Mankato, Minnesota 56002.
www.capstonepress.com

Library of Congress Cataloging-in-Publication Data
Richardson, Adele, 1966–
    Mercury / by Adele Richardson.
    p. cm.—(First facts. The solar system)
    Includes bibliographical references and index.
    ISBN 0-7368-3690-X (hardcover)
    ISBN 0-7368-5170-4 (paperback)
    1. Mercury (Planet)—Juvenile literature. I. Title. II. Series.
QB611.R53 2005
523.41—dc22   2004010936

Summary: Discusses the orbit, surface features, and exploration of the planet Mercury.

Editorial Credits
Christopher Harbo, editor; Juliette Peters, designer and illustrator; Jo Miller, photo researcher;
    Scott Thoms, photo editor

Photo Credits
Astronomical Society of the Pacific/NASA, 14–15
NASA/The Johns Hopkins University Applied Physics Laboratory, 17
NASA/JPL/Northwestern University, 5, 9, 20
Photodisc, cover, 1, 4, planet images within illustrations and chart, 7, 11, 13, 19, 21
Space Images/NASA/JPL, 10
Steven L. Kipp, 16

1 2 3 4 5 6 10 09 08 07 06 05

Table of Contents

Mariner 10 and Mercury

Mercury has been visited by only one spacecraft. *Mariner 10* took pictures of the planet in 1974. The pictures showed a rocky ball covered with **craters**. Scientists thought Mercury looked like Earth's moon.

Fast Facts about Mercury

Diameter: 3,031 miles (4,878 kilometers)

Average Distance from Sun: 36 million miles (58 million kilometers)

Average Temperature (at surface): 801 degrees Fahrenheit (427 degrees Celsius) during the day; minus 279 degrees Fahrenheit (minus 173 degrees Celsius) at night.

Length of Rotation: 59 Earth days

Length of Day: 176 Earth days

Length of Year: 88 Earth days

Moons: None

5

The Solar System

Mercury is the closest planet to the Sun. Venus, Earth, and Mars are the next closest. These planets are mostly made of rock. Jupiter, Saturn, Uranus, and Neptune are the next farthest planets. They are made of gas and ice. Pluto is the farthest planet from the Sun. It is made of rock and ice.

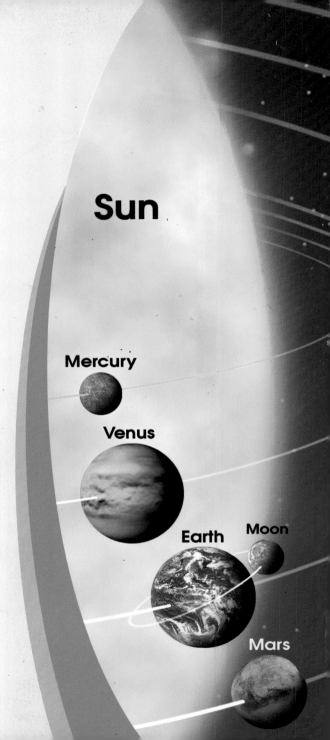

Sun

Mercury

Venus

Earth

Moon

Mars

Jupiter

Saturn

Uranus

Pluto

Neptune

7

Mercury's Lack of Atmosphere

An **atmosphere** is a layer of gases that surrounds a planet. Mercury has no atmosphere. Any gases around Mercury escape into space. Without an atmosphere, the planet's surface is very hot during the day. Mercury's surface is very cold at night.

! Fun Fact!
With no atmosphere, Mercury's sky always looks black, even during the day.

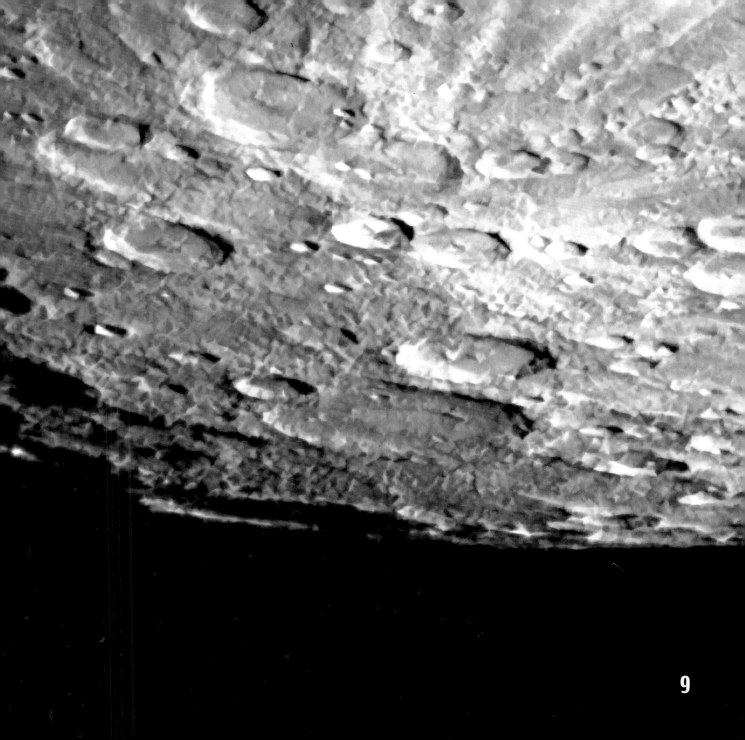

9

Mercury's Makeup

Mercury is made mostly of rock. Its **crust**, or surface, is covered with craters, cliffs, and hills. A rocky **mantle** lies below the crust.

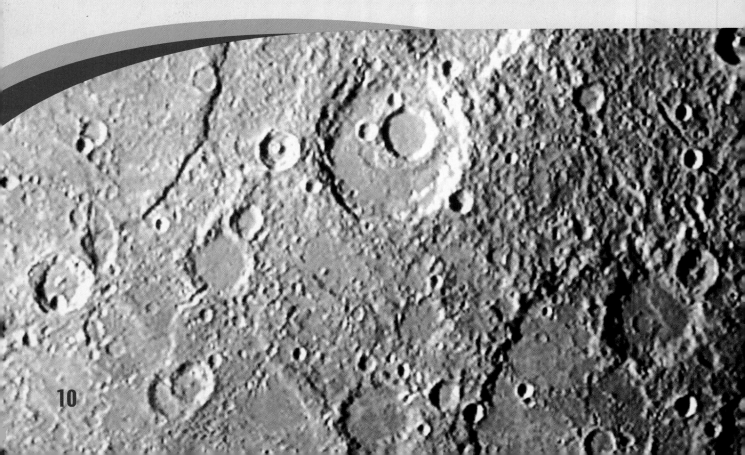

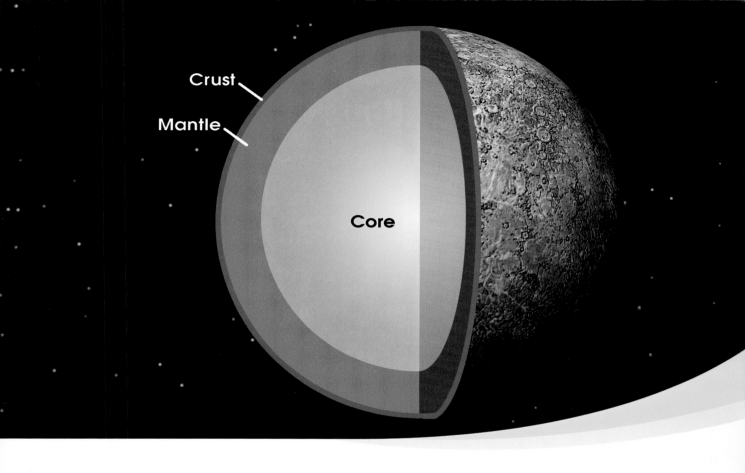

Mercury has a solid iron **core**.
The core makes up most of the planet.
Scientists believe a very thin layer of
melted iron may surround the core.

How Mercury Moves

   Mercury moves in two ways. It quickly circles around the Sun. It also slowly spins on its **axis**. Mercury takes 88 Earth days to circle the Sun once. This period of time is Mercury's year. It takes 59 Earth days to spin around on its axis once.

Fun Fact!

Because Mercury spins so slowly, one day on Mercury (sunrise to sunrise) lasts 176 Earth days. On Mercury, a day is twice as long as a year.

Sun

Mercury

Path around the Sun

Axis

Caloris Basin

The Caloris Basin is a giant crater on Mercury. It is about 810 miles (1,300 kilometers) wide. Scientists believe the crater was made when an **asteroid** smashed into Mercury. The crash also formed hills and mountains.

Fun Fact!
The Caloris Basin is larger than the state of Texas.

Edge of Caloris Basin

Studying Mercury

Mercury is hard to see from Earth. The planet appears low in the sky just before sunrise or just after sunset. People use telescopes to see Mercury at these times.

Mercury

Scientists use spacecraft to study
Mercury. The *Messenger* spacecraft will
arrive at Mercury in 2011. *Messenger*
will circle the planet for one Earth year.

Comparing Mercury to Earth

Mercury and Earth are very different. People could not breathe on Mercury. The planet does not have an atmosphere. People could not live on Mercury either. Its temperatures are too hot during the day and too cold at night.

Fun Fact!
Jupiter and Saturn each have a moon that is bigger than Mercury.

Size Comparison

Earth

Mercury

Amazing but True!

Mercury is a wrinkled planet. Its core was once hotter than it is today. As the core cooled, the planet shrank. Mercury's surface cracked and wrinkled like a raisin. Cliffs and ridges formed on the surface.

Planet Comparison Chart

Planet	Size Rank (1=largest)	Makeup	1 Trip around the Sun (Earth Time)
Mercury	8	rock	88 days
Venus	6	rock	225 days
Earth	5	rock	365 days, 6 hours
Mars	7	rock	687 days
Jupiter	1	gases and ice	11 years, 11 months
Saturn	2	gases and ice	29 years, 6 months
Uranus	3	gases and ice	84 years
Neptune	4	gases and ice	164 years, 10 months
Pluto	9	rock and ice	248 years

Glossary

asteroid (ASS-tuh-roid)—a large rocky body that moves around the Sun; asteroids are too small to be called planets.

atmosphere (AT-muhss-feehr)—the layer of gases that surrounds some planets and moons

axis (AK-siss)—an imaginary line that runs through the middle of a planet; a planet spins on its axis.

core (KOR)—the inner part of a planet that is made of metal or rock

crater (KRAY-tur)—a hole made when an asteroid or a large piece of rock crashes into a planet or moon

crust (KRUHST)—the thin outer layer of a planet's surface

mantle (MAN-tuhl)—the part of a planet between the crust and the core

Read More

Birch, Robin. *Mercury.* Solar System. Philadelphia: Chelsea Clubhouse, 2004.

Rau, Dana Meachen. *Mercury.* Our Solar System. Minneapolis: Compass Point Books, 2002.

Stille, Darlene R. *Mercury.* Our Galaxy and Beyond. Chanhassen, Minn.: Child's World, 2004.

Internet Sites

FactHound offers a safe, fun way to find Internet sites related to this book. All of the sites on FactHound have been researched by our staff.

Here's how:
1. Visit *www.facthound.com*
2. Type in this special code **073683690X** for age-appropriate sites. Or enter a search word related to this book for a more general search.
3. Click on the **Fetch It** button.

FactHound will fetch the best sites for you!

Index

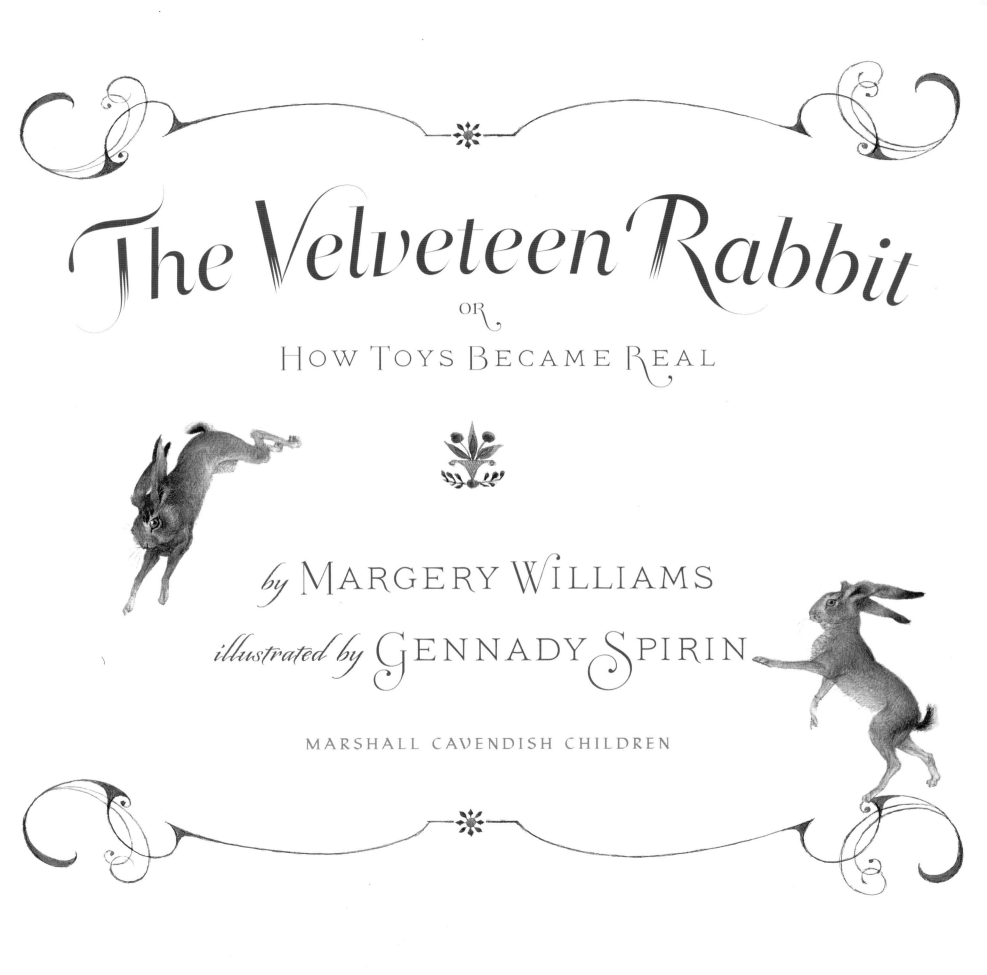

The Velveteen Rabbit

OR

How Toys Became Real

by Margery Williams

illustrated by Gennady Spirin

MARSHALL CAVENDISH CHILDREN

Illustrations copyright © 2011 by Gennady Spirin
All rights reserved
Marshall Cavendish Corporation, 99 White Plains Road, Tarrytown, NY 10591
www.marshallcavendish.us/kids
The illustrations are rendered in watercolor and colored pencil.
Book design by Michael Nelson
Editor: Margery Cuyler
Printed in China [E]
First edition
1 3 5 6 4 2

Marshall Cavendish
Children

To Francesco Bianco from The Velveteen Rabbit
~M. W.

To Nikolai
~G. S.

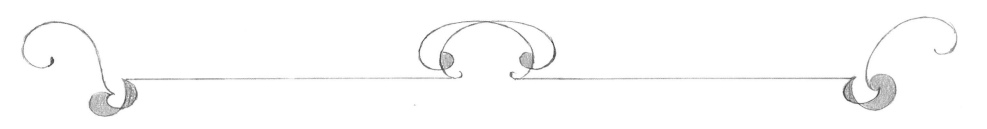

THERE WAS ONCE A VELVETEEN RABBIT, and in the beginning he was really splendid. He was fat and bunchy, as a rabbit should be; his coat was spotted brown and white, he had real thread whiskers, and his ears were lined with pink sateen. On Christmas morning, when he sat wedged in the top of the Boy's stocking with a sprig of holly between his paws, the effect was charming.

There were other things in the stocking, nuts and oranges and a toy engine, and chocolate almonds and a clockwork mouse, but the Rabbit was quite the best of all. For at least two hours the Boy loved him, and then Aunts and Uncles came to dinner, and there was a great rustling of tissue paper and unwrapping of parcels, and in the excitement of looking at all the new presents, the Velveteen Rabbit was forgotten.

For a long time he lived in the toy cupboard or on the nursery floor, and no one thought very much about him. He was naturally shy, and being only made of velveteen, some of the more expensive toys quite snubbed him. The mechanical toys were very superior, and looked down upon everyone else; they were full of modern ideas, and pretended they were real. The model boat, who had lived through two seasons and lost most of his paint, caught the tone from them and never missed an opportunity of referring to his rigging in technical terms. The Rabbit could not claim to be a model of anything, for he didn't know that real rabbits existed; he thought they were all stuffed with sawdust like himself, and he understood that sawdust was quite out-of-date and should never be mentioned in modern circles. Even Timothy, the jointed wooden lion, who was made by the disabled soldiers and should have had

broader views, put on airs and pretended he was connected with Government. Between them all, the poor little Rabbit was made to feel himself very insignificant and commonplace, and the only person who was kind to him at all was the Skin Horse.

The Skin Horse had lived longer in the nursery than any of the others. He was so old that his brown coat was bald in patches and showed the seams underneath, and most of the hairs in his tail had been pulled out to string bead necklaces. He was wise, for he had seen a long succession of mechanical toys arrive to boast and swagger, and by-and-by break their mainsprings and pass away, and he knew that they were only toys and would never turn into anything else. For nursery magic is very strange and wonderful, and only those playthings that are old and wise and experienced like the Skin Horse understand all about it.

"What is REAL?" asked the Rabbit one day, when they were lying side by side near the nursery fender, before Nana came to tidy the room. "Does it mean having things that buzz inside you and a stick-out handle?"

"Real isn't how you are made," said the Skin Horse. "It's a thing that happens to you. When a child loves you for a long, long time, not just to play with, but REALLY loves you, then you become Real."

"Does it hurt?" asked the Rabbit.

"Sometimes," said the Skin Horse, for he was always truthful. "When you are Real, you don't mind being hurt."

"Does it happen all at once, like being wound up," he asked, "or bit by bit?"

"It doesn't happen all at once," said the Skin Horse. "You become. It takes a long time. That's why it doesn't often happen to people who break easily, or have sharp edges, or who have to be carefully kept. Generally, by the

time you are Real, most of your hair has been loved off, and your eyes drop out and you get loose in the joints and very shabby. But these things don't matter at all, because once you are Real, you can't be ugly, except to people who don't understand."

"I suppose you are Real?" said the Rabbit. And then he wished he had not said it, for he thought the Skin Horse might be sensitive. But the Skin Horse only smiled.

"The Boy's Uncle made me Real," he said. "That was a great many years ago; but once you are Real, you can't become unreal again. It lasts for always."

The Rabbit sighed. He thought it would be a long time before this magic called Real happened to him. He longed to become Real, to know what it felt like; and yet the idea of growing shabby and losing his eyes and whiskers was rather sad. He wished that he could become it without these uncomfortable things happening to him.

There was a person called Nana who ruled the nursery. Sometimes she took no notice of the playthings lying about, and sometimes, for no reason whatever, she went swooping about like a great wind and hustled them away in cupboards. She called this "tidying up," and the playthings all hated it, especially the tin ones. The Rabbit didn't mind it so much, for wherever he was thrown, he came down soft.

One evening, when the Boy was going to bed, he couldn't find the china dog that always slept with him. Nana was in a hurry, and it was too much trouble to hunt for china dogs at bedtime, so she simply looked about her, and seeing that the toy cupboard door stood open, she made a swoop.

"Here," she said, "take your old Bunny! He'll do to sleep with you!" And she dragged the Rabbit out by one ear, and put him into the Boy's arms.

That night, and for many nights after, the Velveteen Rabbit slept in the Boy's bed. At first he found it rather uncomfortable, for the Boy hugged him very tight, and sometimes he rolled over on him, and sometimes he pushed him so far under the pillow that the Rabbit could scarcely breathe. And he missed, too, those long moonlight hours in the nursery, when all the house was silent, and his talks with the Skin Horse. But very soon he grew to like it, for the Boy used to talk to him, and made nice tunnels for him under the bedclothes that he said were like the burrows the real rabbits lived in. And they had splendid games together, in whispers, when Nana had gone away to her supper and left the nightlight burning on the mantelpiece. And when the Boy dropped off to sleep, the Rabbit would snuggle down close under his little warm chin and dream, with the Boy's hands clasped close round him all night long.

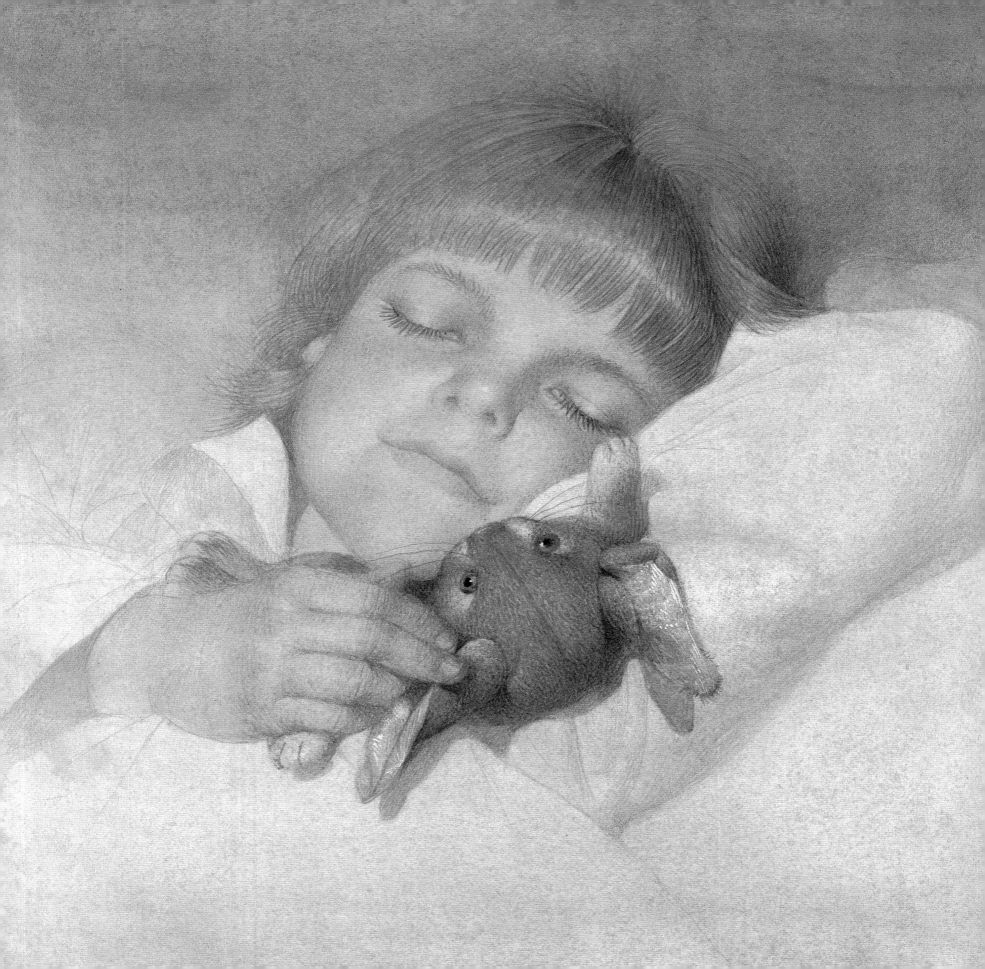

And so time went on, and the little Rabbit was very happy—so happy that he never noticed how his beautiful velveteen fur was getting shabbier and shabbier, and his tail had come unsewn, and all the pink had rubbed off his nose where the Boy had kissed him.

Spring came, and they had long days in the garden, for wherever the Boy went the Rabbit went too. He had rides in the wheelbarrow, and picnics on the grass, and lovely fairy huts built for him under the raspberry canes behind the flower border. And once, when the Boy was called away suddenly to go out to tea, the Rabbit was left out on the lawn until long after dusk, and Nana had to come and look for him with the candle because the Boy couldn't go to sleep unless he was there.

He was wet through with the dew and quite earthy from diving into the burrows the Boy had made for him in the flower bed, and Nana grumbled as she rubbed him off with a corner of her apron.

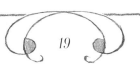

"You must have your old Bunny!" she said. "Fancy all that fuss for a toy!"

The Boy sat up in bed and stretched out his hands.

"Give me my Bunny!" he said. "You mustn't say that. He isn't a toy. He's REAL!"

When the little Rabbit heard that, he was happy, for he knew that what the Skin Horse had said was true at last. The nursery magic had happened to him, and he was a toy no longer. He was Real. The Boy himself had said it.

That night he was almost too happy to sleep, and so much love stirred in his little sawdust heart that it almost burst. And into his boot-button eyes, that had long ago lost their polish, there came a look of wisdom and beauty, so that even Nana noticed it next morning when she picked him up, and said, "I declare if that old Bunny hasn't got quite a knowing expression!"

That was a wonderful summer!

Near the house where they lived there was a wood, and in the long June evenings the Boy liked to go there after tea to play. He took the Velveteen Rabbit with him, and before he wandered off to pick flowers, or play at brigands among the trees, he always made the Rabbit a little nest somewhere among the bracken, where he would be quite cozy, for he was a kind-hearted little boy and he liked Bunny to be comfortable. One evening, while the Rabbit was lying there alone watching the ants that ran to and fro between his velvet paws in the grass, he saw two strange beings creep out of the tall bracken near him.

They were rabbits like himself, but quite furry and brand-new. They must have been very well made, for their seams didn't show at all, and they changed shape in a queer way when they moved; one minute they were long and thin and the next minute fat and bunchy, instead of always staying the same like he did. Their feet padded softly on the ground, and they crept quite close to him, twitching their noses, while the Rabbit stared hard to see which side the clockwork stuck out, for he knew that people who jump generally have something to wind them up. But he couldn't see it. They were evidently a new kind of rabbit altogether.

They stared at him, and the little Rabbit stared back. And all the time their noses twitched.

"Why don't you get up and play with us?" one of them asked.

"I don't feel like it," said the Rabbit, for he didn't want to explain that he had no clockwork.

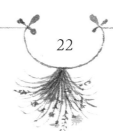

22

"Ho!" said the furry rabbit. "It's as easy as anything." And he gave a big hop sideways and stood on his hind legs.

"I don't believe you can!" he said.

"I can!" said the little Rabbit. "I can jump higher than anything!" He meant when the Boy threw him, but of course he didn't want to say so.

"Can you hop on your hind legs?" asked the furry rabbit.

That was a dreadful question, for the Velveteen Rabbit had no hind legs at all! The back of him was made all in one piece, like a pincushion. He sat still in the bracken and hoped that the other rabbits wouldn't notice.

"I don't want to!" he said again.

But the wild rabbits have very sharp eyes. And this one stretched out his neck and looked.

"He hasn't got any hind legs!" he called out. "Fancy a rabbit without any hind legs!" And he began to laugh.

"I have!" cried the little Rabbit. "I have got hind legs! I am sitting on them!"

"Then stretch them out and show me, like this!" said the wild rabbit. And he began to whirl round and dance, till the little Rabbit got quite dizzy.

"I don't like dancing," he said. "I'd rather sit still!"

But all the while he was longing to dance, for a funny new tickly feeling ran through him, and he felt he would give anything in the world to be able to jump about like these rabbits did.

The strange rabbit stopped dancing and came quite close. He came so close this time that his long whiskers brushed the Velveteen Rabbit's ear, and then he wrinkled his nose suddenly and flattened his ears and jumped backwards.

"He doesn't smell right!" he exclaimed. "He isn't a rabbit at all! He isn't real!"

"I am Real!" said the little Rabbit. "I am Real! The Boy said so!" And he nearly began to cry.

Just then there was a sound of footsteps, and the Boy ran past near them, and with a stamp of feet and a flash of white tails, the two strange rabbits disappeared.

"Come back and play with me!" called the little Rabbit. "Oh, do come back! I know I am Real!"

But there was no answer, only the little ants ran to and fro, and the bracken swayed gently where the two strangers had passed. The Velveteen Rabbit was all alone.

"Oh dear!" he thought. "Why did they run away like that? Why couldn't they stop and talk to me?"

For a long time he lay very still, watching the bracken, and hoping that they would come back. But they never returned, and presently the sun sank lower and the little white moths fluttered out, and the Boy came and carried him home.

Weeks passed, and the little Rabbit grew very old and shabby, but the Boy loved him just as much. He loved him so hard that he loved all his whiskers off, and the pink lining to his ears turned grey, and his brown spots faded. He even began to lose his shape, and he scarcely looked like a rabbit anymore, except to the Boy. To him he was always beautiful, and that was all that the little Rabbit cared about. He didn't mind how he looked to other people, because the nursery magic had made him Real, and when you are Real, shabbiness doesn't matter.

And then, one day, the Boy was ill.

His face grew very flushed, and he talked in his sleep, and his little body was so hot that it burned the Rabbit when he held him close. Strange people came and went in the nursery, and a light burned all night and through it all the little Velveteen Rabbit lay there, hidden from sight under the bedclothes, and he never stirred, for he was afraid that if they found him, someone might take him away, and he knew that the Boy needed him.

It was a long weary time, for the Boy was too ill to play, and the little Rabbit found it rather dull with nothing to do all day long. But he snuggled down patiently and looked forward to the time when the Boy should be well again, and they would go out in the garden amongst the flowers and the butterflies and play splendid games in the raspberry thicket like they used to. All sorts of delightful things he planned, and while the Boy lay half asleep, he crept up close to the pillow and whispered them in his ear. And presently the fever turned, and the Boy got better. He was able to sit up in bed and look at picture books, while the little Rabbit cuddled close at his side. And one day, they let him get up and dress.

It was a bright, sunny morning, and the windows stood wide open. They had carried the Boy out on to the balcony, wrapped in a shawl, and the little Rabbit lay tangled up among the bedclothes, thinking.

The Boy was going to the seaside tomorrow. Everything was arranged, and now it only remained to carry out the doctor's orders. They talked about it all, while the little Rabbit lay under the bedclothes, with just his head peeping out, and listened. The room was to be disinfected, and all the books and toys that the Boy had played with in bed must be burnt.

"Hurrah!" thought the little Rabbit. "Tomorrow we shall go to the seaside!" For the Boy had often talked of the seaside, and he wanted very much to see the big waves coming in, and the tiny crabs, and the sand castles.

Just then Nana caught sight of him.

"How about his old Bunny?" she asked.

"That?" said the doctor. "Why, it's a mass of scarlet fever germs!—Burn it at once. What? Nonsense? Get him a new one. He mustn't have that anymore!"

And so the little Rabbit was put into a sack with the old picture books and a lot of rubbish and carried out to the end of the garden behind the fowl-house. That was a fine place to make a bonfire, only the gardener was too busy just then to attend to it. He had the potatoes to dig and the green peas to gather, but next morning he promised to come quite early and burn the whole lot.

That night the Boy slept in a different bedroom, and he had a new bunny to sleep with him. It was a splendid bunny, all white plush with real glass eyes, but the Boy was too excited to care very much about it. For tomorrow he was going to the seaside, and that in itself was such a wonderful thing that he could think of nothing else.

And while the Boy was asleep, dreaming of the seaside, the little Rabbit lay among the old picture books in the corner behind the fowl-house, and he felt very lonely. The sack had been left untied, and so by wriggling a bit, he was able to get his head through the opening and look out. He was shivering a little, for he had always been used to sleeping in a proper bed, and by this time his coat had worn so thin and threadbare from hugging that it was no longer any protection to him. Nearby he could see the thicket of raspberry canes, growing tall and close like a tropical jungle, in whose shadow he had played with the Boy on bygone mornings. He thought of those long sunlit hours in the garden—how happy they were—and a great sadness came over him. He seemed to see them all pass before him, each more beautiful than the other, the fairy huts in the flower bed, the quiet evenings in the wood when he lay in the bracken and the little ants ran over his paws; the wonderful day when he first knew that he was Real. He thought of the Skin Horse, so wise and gentle, and all that he had told him. Of what use was it to be loved and lose one's beauty and become Real if it all ended like this? And a tear, a real tear, trickled down his little shabby velvet nose and fell to the ground.

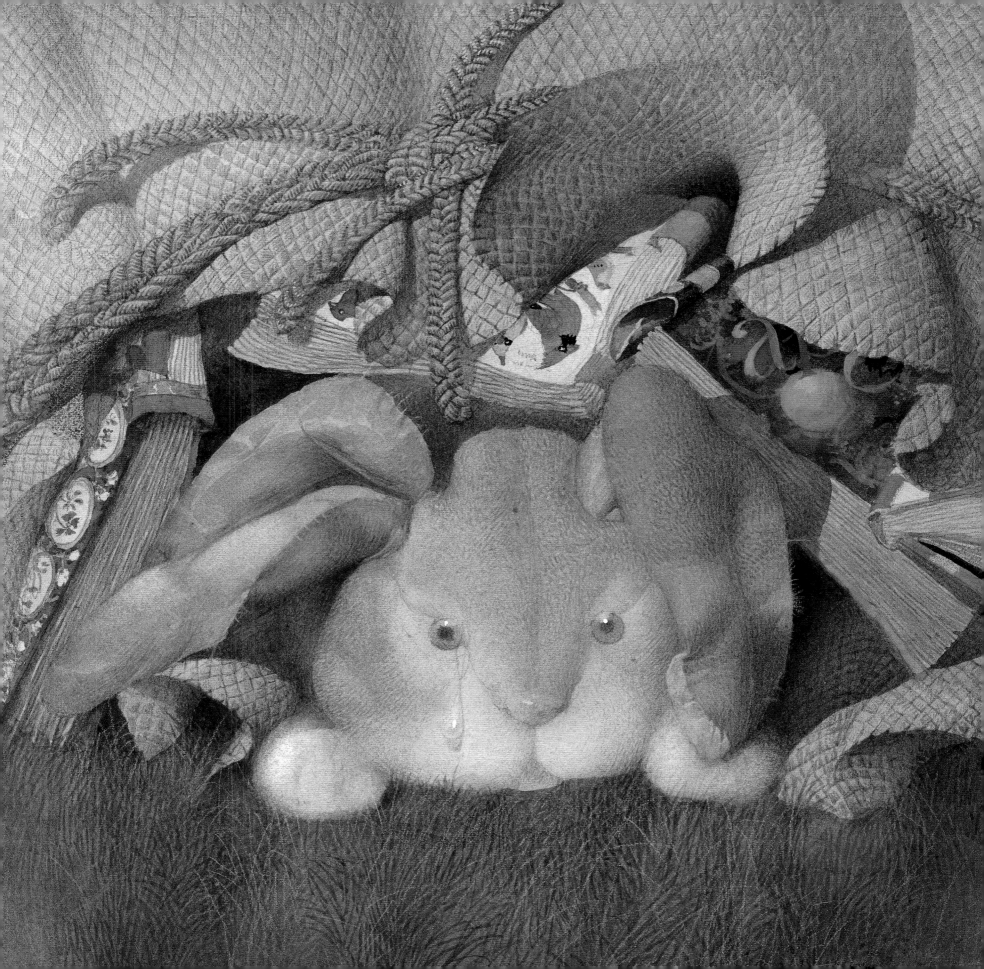

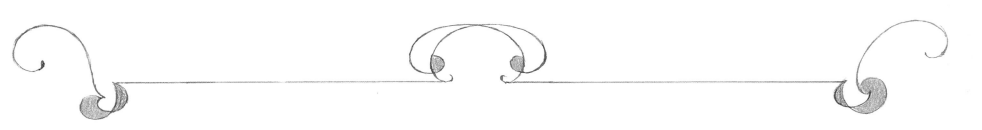

And then a strange thing happened. For where the tear had fallen, a flower grew out of the ground, a mysterious flower, not at all like any that grew in the garden. It had slender green leaves the color of emeralds, and in the center of the leaves a blossom like a golden cup. It was so beautiful that the little Rabbit forgot to cry and just lay there watching it. And presently the blossom opened, and out of it there stepped a fairy.

She was quite the loveliest fairy in the whole world. Her dress was of pearl and dewdrops, and there were flowers round her neck and in her hair, and her face was like the most perfect flower of all. And she came close to the little Rabbit and gathered him up in her arms and kissed him on his velveteen nose that was all damp from crying.

"Little Rabbit," she said, "don't you know who I am?"

The Rabbit looked up at her, and it seemed to him that he had seen her face before, but he couldn't think where.

"I am the nursery magic Fairy," she said. "I take care of all the playthings that the children have loved. When they are old and worn out and the children don't need them anymore, then I come and take them away with me and turn them into Real."

"Wasn't I Real before?" asked the little Rabbit.

"You were Real to the Boy," the Fairy said, "because he loved you. Now you shall be Real to everyone."

And she held the little Rabbit close in her arms and flew with him into the wood.

It was light now, for the moon had risen. All the forest was beautiful, and the fronds of the bracken shone like frosted silver. In the open glade between the tree trunks, the wild rabbits danced with their shadows on the velvet grass, but when they saw the Fairy, they all stopped dancing and stood round in a ring to stare at her.

"I've brought you a new playfellow," the Fairy said. "You must be very kind to him and teach him all he needs to know in Rabbit-land, for he is going to live with you forever and ever!"

And she kissed the little Rabbit again and put him down on the grass.

"Run and play, little Rabbit!" she said.

But the little Rabbit sat quite still for a moment and never moved. For when he saw all the wild rabbits dancing around him, he suddenly remembered about his hind legs, and he didn't want them to see that he was made all in one piece. He did not know that when the Fairy kissed him that last time she had changed him altogether. And he might have sat there a long time, too shy to move, if just then something hadn't tickled his nose, and before he thought what he was doing, he lifted his hind toe to scratch it.

And he found that he actually had hind legs! Instead of dingy velveteen, he had brown fur, soft and shiny, his ears twitched by themselves, and his whiskers were so long that they brushed the grass. He gave one leap and the joy of using those hind legs was so great that he went springing about the turf on them, jumping sideways and whirling round as the others did, and he grew so excited that when at last he did stop to look for the Fairy, she had gone.

He was a Real Rabbit at last, at home with the other rabbits.

Autumn passed and winter, and in the spring, when the days grew warm and sunny, the Boy went out to play in the wood behind the house. And while he was playing, two rabbits crept out from the bracken and peeped at him. One of them was brown all over, but the other had strange markings under his fur, as though long ago he had been spotted, and the spots still showed through. And about his little soft nose and his round black eyes there was something familiar, so that the Boy thought to himself:

"Why, he looks just like my old Bunny that was lost when I had scarlet fever!"

But he never knew that it really was his own Bunny, come back to look at the child who had first helped him to be Real.